ANTONY AND CLEOPATRA

Text and Performance

MICHAEL SCOTT

M
MACMILLAN

First published 1983 by
THE MACMILLAN PRESS LTD
Houndmills, Basingstoke, Hampshire RG21 2XS
and London
Companies and representatives
throughout the world

ISBN 0–333–33997–5

A catalogue record for this book is available
from the British Library.

Printed in China

Reprinted 1993

TEXT AND PERFORMANCE

PUBLISHED

CONTENTS

Illustrations will be found in Part Two

ACKNOWLEDGEMENTS

Quotations of the text of the play are from the New Penguin
Shakespeare edition (1977), edited by Emrys Jones.

Source details for the illustrations are given with the relevant
captions to the photographs.

I am grateful to Dr Gordon Williams of the University of
Wales and Professor Peter Davison of the University of Kent
for reading through the draft of the book. My thanks are due to
members of the library staff at Sunderland Polytechnic,
Newcastle University, Durham University, the Theatre
Museum and the Shakespeare Centre at Stratford-upon-Avon
for their invaluable help. I have made close use of the Prompt
Copy and Stage Manager's Script for the RSC 1978 production,
housed at the Shakespeare Centre, for which I am grateful to
Peter Brook for permission. I have also referred to similar
material for the 1972 production. My thanks are due to
Maurice Daniels at the Royal Shakespeare Theatre for bringing to mind lost incidents in the various productions, and to
Sarah Mahaffy and Derick Mirfin at Macmillan for their
encouraging support of not only this volume but of the 'Text
and Performance' series as a whole. I am grateful to Miss T. M.
O'Reilly who produced the typescript, and as ever to my wife
Eirlys, who helped with the research and has been a pertinent
critic throughout. I dedicate the book to our daughters Jane
and Jennifer.

GENERAL EDITOR'S PREFACE

For many years a mutual suspicion existed between the theatre director and the literary critic of drama. Although in the first half of the century there were important exceptions, such was the rule. A radical change of attitude, however, has taken place over the last thirty years. Critics and directors now increasingly recognise the significance of each other's work and acknowledge their growing awareness of interdependence. Both interpret the same text, but do so according to their different situations and functions. Without the director, the designer and the actor, a play's existence is only partial. They revitalise the text with action, enabling the drama to live fully at each performance. The academic critic investigates the script to elucidate its textual problems, understand its conventions and discover how it operates. He may also propose his view of the work, expounding what he considers to be its significance.

Dramatic texts belong therefore to theatre and to literature. The aim of the 'Text and Performance' series is to achieve a fuller recognition of how both enhance our enjoyment of the play. Each volume follows the same basic pattern. Part One provides a critical introduction to the play under discussion, using the techniques and criteria of the literary critic in examining the manner in which the work operates through language, imagery and action. Part Two takes the enquiry further into the play's theatricality by focusing on selected productions of recent times so as to illustrate points of contrast and comparison in the interpretation of different directors and actors, and to demonstrate how the drama has worked on the modern stage. In this way the series seeks to provide a lively and informative introduction to major plays in their text and performance.

MICHAEL SCOTT

PLOT SYNOPSIS AND SOURCES

Antony, one of the three rulers of the Roman Empire after Julius Caesar's death, has fallen in love with Cleopatra, Queen of Egypt. To force him to return to Rome, his wife Fulvia has waged war on the Empire. The Romans accuse him of dotage in Egypt while Pompey, son of Pompey the Great, also threatens Rome with war. Learning of Fulvia's death, Antony returns to Rome to help his co-emperors, Octavius Caesar and Lepidus, fight Pompey. To strengthen the unity of the triumvirate he agrees to marry Caesar's sister Octavia. At a meeting of the co-emperors peace is concluded with Pompey and feasts arranged; but after Antony has established his new home in Athens, Caesar wages new wars with Pompey and arrests Lepidus. Octavia goes to Rome as Antony's ambassador, but he returns to Egypt and Cleopatra. Octavius pursues him there. On Cleopatra's advice, Antony first fights at sea. In the midst of battle Cleopatra's ship flees and Antony, instead of fighting on, humiliatingly follows her. Octavius Caesar rejects his requests for peace and sends a soldier, Thidias, to Cleopatra with terms of greeting. Antony interrupts their meeting, storms at the Queen for her unfaithfulness, and has Thidias whipped. His friend Enobarbus deserts him for Caesar. A second battle is fought, this time on land, and Antony achieves a limited victory, while Enobarbus, broken-hearted at his treachery, dies. In a third battle Cleopatra's fleet surrenders to Caesar. Antony accuses her of betrayal; she, to pacify him, sends word that she has died. Grief-stricken, he makes to kill himself, after his servant Eros has refused to give him the death-blow. As Antony lies dying, a messenger from Cleopatra tells him that she is not dead but is taking refuge in her monument. Antony is carried to her there, where he dies. Cleopatra, attended by her women, is captured in the monument by Caesar's men. She is secretly informed that, despite his promise of generous treatment, Caesar intends to humiliate her in Rome. A country man arrives and is allowed through to give the Queen figs. His basket, however, contains serpents. Her women array the Queen in her best garments. Iras kisses her and falls dead. Cleopatra puts an asp to her breast, takes another and so dies. Charmian likewise induces a snake-bite and dies as Caesar's soldiers enter. Their leader follows and orders that Cleopatra be buried with her Antony.

Sources

Shakespeare's principal source for the play was Plutarch's *Life of Marcus Antonius*. The historian's *Parallel Lives of the Greeks and Romans* was translated from Greek to French by Jacques Amyot in 1559, and that version was in turn translated into English in 1579 by Sir Thomas North.

PART ONE: TEXT

1 INTRODUCTION

Antony and Cleopatra is Shakespeare's mature epic drama.
Written in 1606/7, its immediate forbears were the four great
tragedies – *Hamlet, Othello, King Lear* and *Macbeth* – and some of
the problem plays, difficult both in structure and in theme:
*Troilus and Cressida, All's Well That Ends Well, Measure for
Measure*. In the tragedies he had presented the fall of great men:
complex individuals conceived with the veracity of psychologi-
cal insight. In the problem plays he had focused on the
structure of society itself. He questioned its conduct, its law and
order by employing the sexual conduct and amorous desires of
individuals as a means to probe institutions and structures
beyond the lovers themselves. In reaching both the tragedies
and the problem plays he had written his English history plays
and his early tragedies, including *Romeo and Juliet* and *Julius
Caesar*, and had reached the heights of romantic and satiric
comedy in plays moving from *Love's Labour's Lost* and *A
Midsummer Night's Dream* to *Twelfth Night* and *As You Like It*.
Such, and more – *The Comedy of Errors, The Taming of the Shrew*,
the *Sonnets* – form the background of a play which has its focus
on the experience of love, not merely in terms of its romance or
its comedy or its tragic result, but on the interplay of two people
alienated by each other, and their political rival, from the world
they should control.

Criticism of *Antony and Cleopatra* has been rich and varied.
Dryden in his version of the story, *All for Love* (1678), gave his
drama the subtitle 'The World Well Lost'; and critics until the
present century were happy to debate the implications of such a
judgement as applied to Shakespeare's work. A. C. Bradley at
the beginning of this century produced the best criticism of this
kind, concluding – in his *Oxford Lectures on Poetry* (1909) – that it
was 'better for the world's sake, and not less for their own, that

they should fail and die'. Bradley, however, noted other aspects
of the play. In particular, he pointed to its immense size and
scope, its 'vast canvas'; and noted that, unlike the four
tragedies, *Antony and Cleopatra* disengages the audience's sym-
pathy. We experience the play with an astonishment rather
than an involvement.

Shakespearean criticism since Bradley has acknowledged his
influence often in its reaction against him. Scholars have
stressed the importance of the poetry and the imagery of the
play which reveals a richer work than one depending on a black
or white moral judgement concerning the conduct of the lovers.
Wilson Knight discovered an intense spirituality in the conclusion of the play; L. C. Knights found the work to be one of
revelation rather than judgement; S. L. Bethell perceived
through the poetry a Cleopatra who was 'not so much a
character as a metaphysical conceit', demonstrating con-
trarieties of experience. David Daiches has seen the work as a
drama about role-play in various human activity and its
relation to true identity, stating that it 'is a play about the ways
of confronting experience, about variety and identity'. Northrop Frye has seen the work not as a moral play but rather one
descriptive of 'the night side of nature'. Terence Hawkes has
studied its language in relation to its spatial image on stage;
and E. A. J. Honigmann has looked at the play's structure in
the way in which it deliberately produces a variety of response
within the audience. Emrys Jones has also concentrated on the
structure of the play, as did the late Ernest Schanzer who
believed it to be Shakespeare's 'problem play *par excellence*'.

These are just some of the many lines which have been taken
through the play. For convenience we term it an epic drama
since it is heroic, episodic and vast. Yet it is also a very intimate
play. It can be seen as tragic or satiric or a combination of the
two. In places it can be comic, in places full of pity and despair
and yet strangely disengaging. In total it allows us to understand rather than to empathise and as such forces us to reflect
on the complex nature of the relationship between Antony,
Cleopatra and the world. The lovers are central to the play and
it is with them therefore that discussion can begin although it
needs to be recognised that their centrality is to a complex
whole.

2 THE QUEEN OF LOVE

To play Cleopatra must be one of the greatest challenges to an actress. She is more difficult than any other Shakespearean female in that, until the final scene, one does not really know what motivates her being; and even in her death questions remain around her. The task then is to act an enigma. Yet in order to do this Shakespeare has given a few clues to his artist. The most significant comes in the last act where the Queen talks of her future in history:

CLEO.   Now, Iras, what think'st thou?
            Thou, an Egyptian puppet, shall be shown
            In Rome as well as I. Mechanic slaves
            With greasy aprons, rules, and hammers shall
            Uplift us to the view. In their thick breaths,
            Rank of gross diet, shall we be enclouded,
            And forced to drink their vapour.
IRAS   The gods forbid!
CLEO.   Nay, 'tis most certain, Iras. Saucy lictors
            Will catch at us like strumpets, and scald rhymers
            Ballad us out o' tune. The quick comedians
            Extemporally will stage us, and present
            Our Alexandrian revels. Antony
            Shall be brought drunken forth, and I shall see
            Some squeaking Cleopatra boy my greatness
            I' th' posture of a whore.   [v ii 207–21]

The actor playing Cleopatra for Shakespeare's company, of course, would have been a boy and the theatre would have been either the Globe or the smaller Blackfriars. At either of them there would have been a lively throng of people around the stage to see Cleopatra's prophecy come at least partly true. Antony earlier is seen drunk on Pompey's galley in imitation of an Alexandrian revel, and from the opening scene Cleopatra is referred to as a 'strumpet', 'ribaudred nag' and 'triple-turned whore'. Thus Cleopatra's words draw attention to elements in her presentation before the Jacobean audience. The dialogue therefore is self-referential and as such demonstrates Shakespeare's confidence in his play and his actor.

More importantly it tells us the author wished his actor to be conscious about his role. Cleopatra comments upon her impersonator and thus distances herself from him. The result is that we briefly see Shakespeare's conception of the Queen in as objective a manner as he can present. There we see her motivating force. Shakespeare's Cleopatra in her regality is so far above the theatre and its audience laughing at the antics of a puppet or a boy comedian that she can hardly contemplate the indignity and certainly not witness it. Thus Shakespeare allows her to alienate herself from the audience and so go to her death with the awe and mystery of the great Queen. The effect is increased by the entrance of the clown who, through his unwitting commentary on her history, again sets the Queen apart as something to be considered in her tragedy. By drawing attention to the charges of whore and drunkard at this point, Shakespeare raises Cleopatra above such levels and instructs his actor how she should be portrayed. Despite all the inconsistencies she is first and foremost a Queen.

The modern actress can still take Shakespeare's advice and focus her attention primarily on Cleopatra's royal nature. It would be too easy for her to present the strumpet or the coquette. She must think as a Queen and entice her Antony from that position. Shakespeare here had taken his cue from Plutarch's account of Cleopatra's first appearance to Antony, a description on which he improves:

> The barge she sat in, like a burnished throne,
> Burned on the water. The poop was beaten gold;
> Purple the sails, and so perfumèd that
> The winds were lovesick with them. The oars were silver,
> Which to the tune of flutes kept stroke and made
> The water which they beat to follow faster,
> As amorous of their strokes. For her person,
> It beggared all description. She did lie
> In her pavilion, cloth-of-gold of tissue,
> O'erpicturing that Venus where we see
> The fancy outwork nature. On each side her
> Stood pretty dimpled boys, like smiling cupids,
> With divers-coloured fans, whose wind did seem
> To glow the delicate cheeks which they did cool,
> And what they undid did.   [II ii 195–210]

(Compare the passage in T. J. B. Spencer, *Shakespeare's Plutarch*, p. 201.)

Although her feminine wiles are ever-present here, the emphasis is on her stature, not merely as a Queen but as a living goddess of love, 'O'erpicturing Venus' herself, sailing down the river to capture the greatest warrior of the world. Cleopatra is not presented as a squeaking boy but as a mysterious deity with an insatiable appetite for love itself:

> Age cannot wither her, nor custom stale
> Her infinite variety. Other women cloy
> The appetites they feed, but she makes hungry
> Where most she satisfies; for vilest things
> Become themselves in her, that the holy priests
> Bless her when she is riggish.   [II ii 240–5]

Cleopatra retains a dignity in flirtation, a regality in coquettishness which sets her apart. It is this immortal quality as a goddess of love, therefore, which frames Shakespeare's conception of the character. With this in mind the actress can begin to study the way in which Shakespeare allows Cleopatra's neo-divinity and regality to have a tangible realism in her feelings for Antony and her pleasure with him. She begins by testing him:

> CLEO. If it be love indeed, tell me how much.
> ANT.   There's beggary in the love that can be reckoned.
> CLEO. I'll set a bourn how far to be beloved.
> ANT.   Then must thou needs find out new heaven, new earth.
>   [I i 14–17]

This is not the talk of the strumpet which Philo has just described. It is the questioning of the enchantress in command of her lover. Perhaps to the outside world they appear foolish – Shakespeare tells us in *As You Like It* [II iv 43–52] that all lovers do so – but here there is the pleasantry of amatory banter. The infatuation however is disturbed by the intrusion of the world. To the Messenger's announcement of news from Rome, Antony responds: 'Grates me! The sum.' [I i 8].

Rome is Cleopatra's enemy – just as, in Keats's great romantic poem *Lamia*, Appollonius proves the enchantress

Lamia's opponent. Rome is the cold world where there are tangible boundaries and regulations ready to encroach on the paradise of love. The messengers from Rome succeed and thus Cleopatra falls to quarrelling with Antony. Act I scene iii shows her insecurity not in terms of love, but of Rome. Her jealousy is not particularly directed against Fulvia, though Antony's wife is made the basis of the argument. Rather it derives from the fear that she might lose Antony to what the Roman messengers signify – the world outside their love. The scene accelerates in temper and quick-fired repartee to the moment when Antony can stand no more. He goes to depart on 'I'll leave you lady' and Cleopatra shows the essence of her nature in the quiet reverence of love:

> Courteous lord, one word.
> Sir, you and I must part, but that's not it.
> Sir, you and I have loved, but there's not it.
> That you know well. Something it is I would –
> O, my oblivion is a very Antony,
> And I am all forgotten.   [I iii 86–91]

For the audience Antony's answer is pertinent for it forces us back from Cleopatra's depth of emotion by giving a tender commentary upon it:

> But that your royalty
> Holds idleness your subject, I should take you
> For idleness itself.   [I iii 91–3]

Her royalty is above all the ability to control idleness and love itself. Shakespeare carries the nature of the relationship above the normal modes of argument and reconciliation to a moment of intimate simplicity. As she briefly replies, the silence of an embrace is demanded until with an effort of will she re-introduces the antithetical world of responsibility. Thus a loving tender explanation is followed by a concentration on duty:

> But, sir, forgive me,
> Since my becomings kill me when they do not
> Eye well to you. Your honour calls you hence.

> Therefore be deaf to my unpitied folly,
> And all the gods go with you! ...   [i iii 95–9]

It is from a scene such as this, revealing the intimacy of her love, that the coquettishness and even faithfulness during the rest of the action can be understood. Her passions, it seems, are disguised in her love games. Some critics, however, would disagree – Honigmann stating for example: 'We often wonder whether she is interested in love for its own sake, or whether she merely needs it as a pretext for posing in amusing new attitudes' (*Shakespeare: Seven Tragedies*, p. 163).

Such in fact is Shakespeare's concept of Antony's fear. In his eyes Cleopatra betrays him in the latter part of the play on three occasions. The first is when she leaves the sea battle; the second when she entertains Thidias with courtesy; and the third when her fleet surrenders to Caesar. On the first of these occasions, the dramatist's explanation for her can be taken at face value:

> O my lord, my lord,
> Forgive my fearful sails! I little thought
> You would have followed.   [iii xi 54–6]

Quite simply, in the context of the fight for which she was largely responsible Cleopatra proved to be a coward.

On the second occasion, however, Shakespeare gives an ambiguity to her words to Thidias and capitalises on this by making Enobarbus show concern:

THID. He [Caesar] knows that you embraced not Antony
       As you did love, but as you feared him.
CLEO.   O!
THID. The scars upon your honour therefore he
       Does pity, as contrainèd blemishes,
       Not as deserved.
CLEO.   He is a god, and knows
       What is most right. Mine honour was not yielded,
       But conquered merely.
ENOB. (*aside*)   To be sure of that,
       I will ask Antony. Sir, sir, thou art so leaky
       That we must leave thee to thy sinking, for
       Thy dearest quit thee.   [iii xiii 56–65]

Part of the ambiguity must lie with Cleopatra's exclamation
'O!'. The actress has to make a decision. Is this woman
indignant, surprised, meditative, ashamed or what? The
interpretation given must prepare not only for her following
lines but for those also of Enobarbus. That Antony's friend
leaves the stage to find him, showing distrust in Cleopatra,
signifies that Shakespeare wished her words to be uttered
without any recognisable satire – unless, of course, the
dramatist wished us to regard Enobarbus as a mere trouble-
maker. As the scene continues Cleopatra's words make matters
clearer. It appears that her pride in her feminine power is being
displayed in order to encourage Thidias:

> Most kind messenger,
> Say to great Caesar this: in deputation
> I kiss his conquering hand. Tell him I am prompt
> To lay my crown at's feet, and there to kneel,
> Till from his all-obeying breath I hear
> The doom of Egypt.   [III xiii 73–8]

What, Shakespeare wishes us to ask, is the nature of this
enticement? Certainly Cleopatra is portrayed as becoming
more intimate, taking pleasure in the pride of memory, as
Thidias bestows his kiss:

> Your Caesar's father oft,
> When he hath mused of taking kingdoms in,
> Bestowed his lips on that unworthy place,
> As it rained kisses.   [82–5]

The 'rains' which now come are, of course, those of Antony's
rage. The importance of his outburst, however, lies not merely
in his words but also in Cleopatra's silence. For over twenty
lines she says nothing while with the court she witnesses his
anger. Indignantly she then attempts to quieten him, 'Good my
lord –' but is silenced. For the next fifty lines she is allowed only
similar frustrated questions and interjections: 'O, is't come to
this?'; 'Wherefore is this?'; 'Have you done yet?'; 'I must stay
his time'; 'Not know me yet?'.

It is the last question which places the scene. Some may like
to read from all that has gone before a confession of unfaithful-

ness, but her irritation and confusion with Antony seem to find their resolution in 'Not know me yet?'. It is a confession of her nature, not of a mortal sin against her lover. The question asks Antony why he cannot understand that she was teasing Thidias to gratify her pride, her royalty, her neo-deity as the Queen of Love, but not to betray her relationship with him. This Queen naturally plays, flirts and teases, but the constancy of her relationship depends on her knowledge of her partner. Caesar and his camp merely 'word' Cleopatra – as Shakespeare later has her explain at Caesar's departure from the monument, 'He words me, girls, he words me . . .' [v ii 191] – whereas Antony loves her.

Yet for Shakespeare's Antony such frivolity in Cleopatra can lead only to mistrust and betrayal. It is this which is confirmed when her ships surrender to Octavius. In confusion Antony confesses then to his servant that he cannot understand her ways and as such has no identity:

> . . .   Here I am Antony,
> Yet cannot hold this visible shape, my knave.
> I made these wars for Egypt; and the Queen –
> Whose heart I thought I had, for she had mine,
> Which, whilst it was mine, had annexed unto 't
> A million more, now lost – she, Eros, has
> Packed cards with Caesar, and false-played my glory
> Unto an enemy's triumph.   [iv xiv 13–20]

Shakespeare allows his Antony plenty of reason to think this of the Queen. Her tricks, her coquettishness, her frivolity, her changing moods, her adherence to a code of lightness and love – all add to an impression of frivolity. But the dramatist underpins this portrayal with moments of depth. Small instances of her integrity show through her love-games at key moments – as with 'Courteous lord, one word', or 'Not know me yet?'; or as with the despairing, unbelieving three-word question repeated to the messenger in the midst of her tirade, 'He is married?' [ii v 97, 98], or with her confession of cowardice and lack of knowledge at the first betrayal, 'I little thought / You would have followed' [iii xi 55–6]. Such brief insights can go almost unnoticed, but they are ever-present,

establishing the integrity of the Queen and preparing for her
tragic realisation of Antony's death:

> Noblest of men, woo't die?
> Hast thou no care of me? Shall I abide
> In this dull world, which in thy absence is
> No better than a sty? O, see, my women,
> *(Antony dies)*
> The crown o' th' earth doth melt. My lord!
> O, withered is the garland of the war,
> The soldier's pole is fall'n; young boys and girls
> Are level now with men. The odds is gone,
> And there is nothing left remarkable
> Beneath the visiting moon.   [IV xv 59–68]

In face of the cruel reality of the cold world Cleopatra's
frivolous world of love, an Egyptian temple of Venus, can bear
no credence. Her attitude to Caesar on his arrival at the
monument is characteristically one of deception. The much-
debated Seleucus episode, as we shall see below, seems an
element of her deceit taken straight from Plutarch's account.
The Emperor finds it all mildly amusing but he and Cleopatra
have no foundations for communication. His entry to the
monument signifies the end of an age of love, ephemera and
dreams, as she tells Dolabella:

> I dreamt there was an emperor Antony.
> O, such another sleep, that I might see
> But such another man!   [v ii 76–8]

That sleep cannot be with Caesar, rather it has to be her death:
a final orgasmic act. The asp sucks at her breast and brings her
enigmatic world of love to a close.

3   THE DIVIDED SELF

If Cleopatra is of the order of Venus, Antony is of that of Mars
and it is within the natural conflict of these deities that the
tragedy lies. The relationship with the gods is constantly
brought to mind through the language of the play – for
example, her quizzing of Mardian, the eunuch:

CLEO.	Hast thou affections?
MARD.	Yes, gracious madam.
CLEO.	Indeed?
MARD.	Not in deed, madam; for I can do nothing
	But what indeed is honest to be done.
	Yet have I fierce affections, and think
	What Venus did with Mars.
CLEO.	O, Charmian,
	Where think'st thou he is now? . . . [I v 12–18]

Cleopatra takes Mardian's words and immediately applies
them to her love for Antony whose eyes, as Philo tells us in the
first passage of the play, 'Have glowed like plated Mars' [I i 4].
Yet it is Philo who, in opening the drama, has suggested that
this Mars of men has lost his warlike aspect and 'become the
bellows and the fan / To cool a gipsy's lust' [I i 9–10].
Antony's difficulties lie throughout in a conflict of loyalty. Mars
may love Venus but the nature of the godheads, war and love,
are incompatible.

The conflict of Mars and Venus is demonstrated in
Chaucer's poem, *The Knight's Tale*, which was well known to
Shakespeare. In this Canterbury tale Duke Theseus orders
three altars to be built on the perimeter of a tournament ground
where two brothers, Arcite and Palamon, are to fight for the
love of a chaste lady, Emily. One of these altars is dedicated to
Diana, the goddess of chastity, one to Mars, god of war, and one
to Venus, goddess of love. To each come the respective devotees
to pray for success, Emily to Diana, Palamon to Venus and
Arcite to Mars. Love's triangle is established with Mars in
confrontation with Venus for the victory of the respective

lovers. Saturn is appealed to by the gods to make the final decision. His answer is of dread –

> 'My deere doghter Venus', quod Saturne,
> 'My cours, that hath so wyde for to turne,
> Hath moore power than woot any man.
> Myn is the drenchyng in the see so wan;
> Myn is the prison in the derke cote;
> Myn is the stranglyng and hangyng by the throte'

– and yet of paradoxical hope,

> '. . . weep namoore, I shall doon diligence
> That Palamon, that is thyn owene knyght,
> Shal have his lady, as thou hast him hyght.
> Though Mars shal helpe his knyght, yet nathelees . . .'.
> (*The Knight's Tale*, 2453–8, 2470–3: *Works*, ed. F. N. Robinson, 1957,
> p. 41.)

Saturn's dark diligence and solution to the problem is to allow Arcite victory in battle but to throw him from his horse during the celebratory parade. Arcite dies and Emily is awarded to the distraught Palamon. The gods of war and love are consequently appeased although each of the devotees suffered through the contest.

This story is very different from *Antony and Cleopatra* but elements within it may help us to find some insights into the protagonists' relationship. In the Chaucerian poem, love, honour, war, duty and modesty encircle one another in an attempt to make some sense out of the process of living. The same is true of Shakespeare's story. Antony's tragedy, if such it be, is that he attempts to serve two gods, Mars and Venus. Mars demands a devotion to honour, duty and courage whilst Venus seeks for rest, wantonness and pleasure. This is made clear in the opening scene where skilfully Shakespeare demonstrates Mars's relationship with Venus by allowing Cleopatra to taunt Antony in terms of honour and the soldier to reply in terms of love:

> CLEO. You must not stay here longer. Your dismission
> Is come from Caesar. Therefore hear it, Antony.

> Where's Fulvia's process? Caesar's I would say! Both!
> Call in the messengers. As I am Egypt's Queen,
> Thou blushest, Antony, and that blood of thine
> Is Caesar's homager; else so thy cheeks pay shame
> When shrill-tongued Fulvia scolds. The messengers!

ANT.   Let Rome in Tiber melt, and the wide arch
> Of the ranged empire fall! Here is my space.
> Kingdoms are clay. Our dungy earth alike
> Feeds beast as man. The nobleness of life
> Is to do thus – when such a mutual pair
> And such a twain can do't, in which I bind,
> On pain of punishment, the world to weet
> We stand up peerless.   [i i 26–40]

This is a complex Shakespearean exchange. In an attempt to keep her hold on Antony, Cleopatra is made to attack him in the vulnerability of his pride. She implies that, instead of being master of the world, he is a subject both to Fulvia and to Caesar, and capitalises on the implication by claiming to read in his blushes the truth of her words. She consequently places him in an impossible position. If he follows the dictates of duty and hears the messengers, he will be humiliated. But duty is his veritable obligation as a triumvir of the world. Shakespeare makes Antony logically follow in response, since he now attacks the foundation of his authority. Rome, the empire, kingdoms, power are nothing in comparison with love itself. Antony's terms of reference, his source of identity, is shifted. Nobility now lies with Venus rather than with Mars, with kisses and caresses rather than with arms and a political authority. Thus, when later Antony is placed in the context of war we find that he has to fight according to a new code of behaviour as Canidius comments,

> . . .   his whole action grows
> Not in the power on't. So our leader's led,
> And we are women's men.   [III vii 68–70]

Thus Shakespeare polarises the conflict of love and honour in order to create a theatrical tragedy. He would have known, however, that historically the situation was not as clear cut as this. Plutarch makes it evident that Cleopatra was the culmination of Antony's debauched life, bringing out the worst in him, but nevertheless not its cause:

> Now the government of these Triumviri grew odious and hateful to the Romans, for divers respects. But they most blamed Antonius, because he, being elder than Caesar and of more power and force than Lepidus, gave himself again to his former riot and excess when he left to deal in the affairs of the commonwealth. But, setting aside the ill name he had for insolency, he was yet much more hated in respect of the house he dwelt in, the which was the house of Pompey the Great, a man as famous for his temperance, modesty, and civil life, as for his three Triumphs. For it grieved them to see the gates commonly shut against the captains, magistrates of the city, and also ambassadors of strange nations, which were some-times thrust from the gate with violence; and that the house within was full of tumblers, antic dancers, jugglers, players, jesters, and drunkards, quaffing and guzzling, and that on them he spent and bestowed the most part of his money he got by all kind of possible extortions, bribery and policy. . . .
>
> Antonius being thus inclined, the last and extremist mischief of all other (to wit, the love of Cleopatra) lighted on him, who did waken and stir up many vices yet hidden in him, and were never seen to any; and, if any spark of goodness or hope of rising were left in him, Cleopatra quenched it straight and made it worse than before.
>
> *(Shakespeare's Plutarch*, pp. 195, 199.)

Plutarch's Antony, then, is a slave to the god of wine, Bacchus, well before Cleopatra enters the scene; but Shakespeare hardly mentions the fact. Bacchus is evoked in the play only in the re-creation of an Egyptian Bacchanal on Pompey's ship; while Enobarbus gives just one indication that Antony is naturally licentious when he tells Menas why the Emperor will leave Octavia for Egypt [II vi 123]. Otherwise the focus is on the heroic nature – also found in Plutarch – of Antony's past in relation to the lasciviousness that Egypt has brought about.

In taking the emphasis away from Bacchus and placing it on Mars, Shakespeare introduces another god, Hercules, to emphasise not only Antony's strength but his decline from masculine honour. In his description of Antony Plutarch noted the emperor's loyalty to Hercules, his 'ancestor':

[Antony] had a noble presence and showed a countenance of one of a noble house. He had a good thick beard, a broad forehead, crook-nosed; and there appeared such a manly look in his countenance as is commonly seen in Hercules' pictures, stamped or graven in metal. Now it had been a speech of old time that the family of the Antonii were descended from one Anton, the son of Hercules, whereof the family took name. This opinion did Antonius seek to confirm in all his doings, not only resembling him in the likeness of his body, as we have said before, but also in wearing of his garments. . . .

(Shakespeare's Plutarch, p. 177.)

Of the many stories concerning the exploits and travels of Hercules, two seem to be of interest in relation to Shakespeare's concept of Antony. The first is that, while in the service of the widow Omphale, Queen of Lydia, Hercules was reported as becoming effeminate to the extent of dressing up as a woman. As has been noted before (see, for example, Northrop Frye and Maurice Charney), Shakespeare capitalises on this story by making an implicit comparison with Antony's situation in Egypt where Cleopatra

> . . .   drunk him to his bed;
> Then put my tires and mantles on him, whilst
> I wore his sword Philippan.   [II v 21–3]

Shakespeare's second allusion to Hercules is more specific. In order to keep her love faithful, Hercules's wife, Deianira, sent Lichas to him with a shirt dipped in the blood of the centaur, Nessus. Hercules had previously killed Nessus with a poisoned arrow when the centaur had attacked Deianira. As Nessus died he had told Deianira that his blood would preserve her husband's love – thus the gift. Hercules in wearing the shirt was poisoned. In his rage he threw Lichas high into the air and to the sea and tore his shirt from his own body pulling with it his flesh. Deianira, seeing what she had done, killed herself and Hercules built a fire on which he sacrificed himself. Ironically therefore, in Deianira's attempt to keep love secure, the Nessus shirt destroyed both wife and husband. The parallel with Antony is plain. When Cleopatra's fleet surrenders to

Octavius, all Antony can see is her betrayal and the cruel irony
that in loving her he has destroyed himself:

>   Eros, ho!
> The shirt of Nessus is upon me. Teach me,
> Alcides, thou mine ancestor, thy rage.
> Let me lodge Lichas on the horns o' th' moon,
> And with those hands that grasped the heaviest club
> Subdue my worthiest self. . . .   [IV xii 42–7]

There is, however, a further irony here for, in calling out to his
servant, Antony evokes the name of the Greek god of love, Eros.
This is the name that Plutarch gives the boy and it is
conveniently kept by Shakespeare since Eros, often as blind
Cupid, is depicted throughout art and literature as the
companion of Venus. The god of love is called upon therefore,
as is the founder of Antony's family (Alcides-Hercules), but it is
love that is now in control of Antony's fate. Hercules, as the
soldiers report in IV iii, has already departed from him leaving
Eros and Cleopatra 'to arm' him in IV iv. It is Venus, not Mars,
that now conducts the remaining course of his life. Defeat in
battle is the immediate result, but the experience of love is
crueller in its ambiguity than the clarity of defeat.

In love what seems betrayal may be faithfulness, what
appears as reality may be illusion since, as stated at the opening
of the play, there can be no reckoning nor boundary to its
province. Cleopatra reports that she is dead, Eros refuses to kill
his master and so destroys himself. Antony, whose training has
been at the hands of Mars not Venus, can hardly understand
such ways and even in his death still tries to instruct Cleopatra
according to his former code:

>   Gentle, hear me:
> None about Caesar trust but Proculeius.   [IV xv 47–8]

It is a final irony as events go on to prove and as Shakespeare
has Cleopatra foretell:

> My resolution and my hands I'll trust,
> None about Caesar.   [49–50]

Cleopatra can trust no soldier in the service of Mars (or Caesar) unless he is prepared, like Antony tried, to join the order of Venus. Thus Antony dies unsure and deluded, conjuring up only the glory of his past in the face of present misery:

> The miserable change now at my end
> Lament nor sorrow at, but please your thoughts
> In feeding them with those my former fortunes,
> Wherein I lived; the greatest prince o' th' world,
> The noblest; and do now not basely die,
> Not cowardly put off my helmet to
> My countryman; a Roman, by a Roman
> Valiantly vanquished. . . .   [51–8]

Such a change was brought about by the incompatibility of the protagonists' allegiances to their varying deities, love and war. Thus his death seals a complex theatrical image. In her distress, Cleopatra hardly allows Antony a word, crying out her love for him; but it is a shout of impotence. Shakespeare has presented the manner in which the 'garland of the war' was 'withered' through the power of love.

4   THE PARADOX OF EXPERIENCE

The critical debate concerning whether the play proves tragic or not is in one sense inexhaustible. What is important, however, is the line taken by recent critics in stating that Shakespeare's aim has been to give an expression of the lovers' experience rather than a sympathetic engagement with it.

Shakespeare's art in the play is comparable with that of a painter. He vividly colours his canvas and juxtaposes various images against each other. A. C. Bradley and, recently, Jonathan Miller have suggested that this is attempted in terms of painters such as Veronese; but we might no less appropriately think of a more modern artist such as Picasso. Much modern art gains its power through swift contrast and distortion. Picasso, for example, will place images in incongruous

situations: birds will be seen in fish bowls, fish in bird cages;
features will be disfigured and lines extended, while colours –
browns, blues, greens – will be starkly placed one against
another with the harshness of line rather than with the
harmony of immediately perceptible nature. Shakespeare's
Antony and Cleopatra works in a similar manner. Consequently,
criticism which sees such contrasts in terms merely of moral
polarities – lascivious Egypt against cold Rome – inevitably
appears to be a misreading of a complex whole. Terence
Hawkes notes,

> It is not that 'love' resides in Egypt, 'all' in Rome, or some such
> sentimental disposition of the demands of existence, but that the
> distinction itself is a false one, because too readily reductive of the
> complications of human experience. Life demands no uncom-
> pounded choice between Egypt and Rome, 'love' and 'all'. It would
> be simple if it did.
>
> (*Shakespeare's Talking Animals*, p. 179.)

In structural terms there is the simplicity of a polarity – on the
one side Mars and on the other Venus – as we have seen, but
this simplicity is compounded by the experience of the choices
being made. In *The Knight's Tale* Saturn talks of his dread
nature, and the reconciliation between the gods is accomp-
lished through distraction and pain. Antony and Cleopatra
discover in their deaths a unity where together they lie
according to the dictates of both Venus and Mars. Their story
on one level concludes with honour and romance, but on
another it ends with realism. Antony dies deluded, Cleopatra
not with a baby at her breast but an asp poisoning her life away.
It is this element of contrast rather than moral judgement
which informs the whole play. Thus Enobarbus tells us of
Cleopatra's attendant,

> Alexas did revolt and went to Jewry on
> Affairs of Antony; there did dissuade
> Great Herod to incline himself to Caesar
> And leave his master Antony. For this pains
> Caesar hath hanged him. . . .   [IV vi 12–16]

We might speculate why Caesar 'hanged him' and, adapting a

line from *The Revenger's Tragedy*, conclude that it was sound policy by the Emperor: 'You that would betray him would betray me.' More important, however, would be to look at the nature of Alexas's revolt and that of Enobarbus as reflective of the experience of the central lovers. Enobarbus expresses the dilemma:

> Mine honesty and I begin to square.
> The loyalty well held to fools does make
> Our faith mere folly. Yet he that can endure
> To follow with allegiance a fallen lord
> Does conquer him that did his master conquer
> And earns a place i' th' story. [III xiii 41–6]

What is the experience of honesty? Do you stand by and see your purpose of life transformed? Enobarbus's last words in Antony's camp are,

> . . .   For shame,
> Transform us not to women. [IV ii 35–6]

Or do you constantly re-evaluate the purpose of life? Experience shows that polarities are false. The ground is ever changing, so that a character might think that, in betraying one falling master by turning to a rising one, he will gain credence; but the reality is that he will be hanged. There is no certainty in existence whether the conduct of love, politics or loyalty is being followed. In the circumstances of defeat Antony can wish sincerely to live 'A private man in Athens' [III xii 15], but for how long would that last? Enobarbus can attempt to prevent his 'faith' and 'honesty' from being 'mere folly' but the reality will be disgrace:

> . . .   O Antony
> Nobler than my revolt is infamous,
> Forgive me in thine own particular,
> But let the world rank me in register
> A master-leaver and a fugitive
> O Antony! O Antony! [IV ix 18–23]

Paradoxically, however, Shakespeare in giving Enobarbus this scene counters the character's words by ennobling him through them. Enobarbus 'earns a place i' th' story' since the ground of experience has again shifted. Antony dies deluded in the arms of Cleopatra. The statement in itself is a paradox since he is with his love and yet has been deluded by her. As in a painting where one colour or figure contrasts with another, so the Enobarbus episode enriches Antony's death-scene, enabling the audience by comparison and contrast to come to terms with the overall image of the play.

Octavius Caesar has a similar function. The Roman world is often depicted on stage as black and white in comparison with the luxurious colours of Egypt, but that is not to imply a simplistic moral judgement. Octavius is presented as a shrewd politician and soldier who sees Antony as a constant threat; but there are elements within his characterisation of warmth and understanding which tend to function similarly to those moments in Cleopatra's history where she reveals the depth of her love. Thus Octavia is blatantly employed by Octavius as a political instrument to triumph over his adversary, but in her farewell brings tears to Caesar's eyes – a fact drawn to our attention by the dramatist, through the satirical asides of the onlooking soldiers, Enobarbus and Agrippa:

ENOB. Will Caesar weep?
AGRI.   He has a cloud in's face.
ENOB. He were the worse for that, were he a horse;
        So is he, being a man.
AGRI.   Why, Enobarbus,
        When Antony found Julius Caesar dead,
        He cried almost to roaring; and he wept
        When at Philippi he found Brutus slain.
ENOB. That year indeed he was troubled with a rheum.
        What willingly he did confound he wailed,
        Believe't, till I wept too.   [III ii 50–9]

To the soldiers Caesar's tears imply weakness. Darkness on the face of a horse rather than a white star denoted imperfection; so do the Emperor's tears, signifying for Enobarbus that Octavius is merely a man. Despite all the images or conceits, in a mortal world there is nothing special, nothing divine with Caesar or Antony since they also experience the vicissitudes of life even in their power. In another context Shakespeare expressed the insight through the defeated leader himself, King Richard, about to be deposed, saying to his companions:

> . . . you have but mistook me all this while.
> I live with bread like you, feel want,
> Taste grief, need friends; subjected thus,
> How can you say to me I am a king?   [*R. II*, III ii 174–7]

Thus it is of all leaders. However much they may think themselves to be of the gods – Mars, Venus, Jove – in truth they are as all men. It is this experience of the human condition in relation to illusions, ambitions and power which confuses Antony, confounds Cleopatra and leaves Caesar in tears at Antony's death:

> O Antony,
> I have followed thee to this. But we do launch
> Diseases in our bodies. I must perforce
> Have shown to thee such a declining day
> Or look on thine. We could not stall together
> In the whole world. But yet let me lament
> With tears as sovereign as the blood of hearts
> That thou, my brother, my competitor
> In top of all design, my mate in empire,
> Friend and companion in the front of war,
> The arm of mine own body, and the heart
> Where mine his thoughts did kindle – that our stars,
> Unreconciliable, should divide
> Our equalness to this. . . .   [v i 35–48]

This is the reflective Octavius, sorrowful but knowledgeable. Within triumph there is a sense of loss of that element that inspired the torment and fuelled the success. Shakespeare's creation of Octavius therefore is not one of a mechanical puppet employed merely as an antagonist to Antony, setting him up for defeat, but as a character like the lovers, who feels the experience of change, of the progress of living. From the moment of his first appearance [I iv], he displays temper, longing, desire, sadness, duplicity, ambition and love: elements which, in a different context, may also be seen in the protagonists themselves. Even Caesar on Pompey's ship gets drunk, although it is he who brings the festivities to a close, while Pompey refuses the chance to be ruler of the world.

Such are the paradoxes of experience depicted on Shakespeare's canvas: soldiers complain, courtiers flirt, rulers take decisions, friends desert, lovers love; but each activity affects another and is affected by others until, in conclusion, death (in Chaucer's words) proves 'an ende of every worldly soore'.

5   CLEOPATRA'S DEATH: Commentary on Act v Scene ii

The final scene of *Antony and Cleopatra* is crucial in bringing together the theme, purpose and theatricality that have pervaded the work. At the beginning of the century, George Bernard Shaw, reacting against romantic interpretations, condemned the scene as sentimentally unrealistic. 'Shakespear', he says, 'finally strains all his huge command of rhetoric and stage pathos to give a theatrical sublimity to the wretched end of the business, and to persuade foolish spectators that the world was well lost by the twain' (Preface, *Three Plays for Puritans*, Penguin edition, p. 29). In the light of subsequent criticism and the insight of twentieth-century dramatic theory, Shaw's view can be challenged as a misreading of the particular episode and consequently of the whole play. The epic quality of the drama ensures that the final scene neither lapses into sentimentality nor fosters an undue empathy between the audience and the stage. Throughout *Antony and Cleopatra* Shakespeare's art has been episodic, and this is continued in v ii which can be divided into five contrasting phases: Proculeius and Dolabella; Caesar and Seleucus; Clown; Death; Epilogue.

Phase 1: Proculeius and Dolabella

The first phase opens with what we might consider as an almost operatic aria [lines 1–8] from the Queen, fittingly stating the paradox of sorrow and resolve. The word 'desolation' sets the tone. The scene is to be of loneliness, barrenness, sorrow. Although her ladies are with her, she is effectively isolated, friendless and powerless in an inhospitable world. Yet this realisation of being alone results not in distraction but contemplation. Caesar's condition is 'paltry', worthless, as refuse, since he is but a menial ('knave') of Fortune. He is the jack in Fortune's pack of cards, the servant-soldier of her desire; but Cleopatra has the trump card, the final hand to play which will defeat Fortune and Caesar, and outweigh all previous deeds. Her thoughts are entirely of 'death', which she describes as a bolt and shackle confining both accident and change to its will of sleep. Death never allows the taste and relish of the earth (dung), which feeds (nurse) both the great (Caesar) and the small (beggar). The obscure word 'palates' here in juxtaposition with 'dung' and 'nurse' helps build the complexity of feeling. 'Dung', though referring to earth, does so with the connotation of manure; 'palates' is a revolving of taste in the mouth, and 'nurse' produces the image of life-giving food. Together the three words encapsulate the existence of life itself for all men: an experience which death alone can obliterate in unconsciousness. Cleopatra's aria is strong and determined; but, by concluding with the name Caesar preceded by this oddly grotesque collocation of 'palates' and 'dung', it also provides a hint of bitterness within the 'better life'. Cleopatra is unsure in her new philosophy since it is not one freely chosen but forced upon her by Fortune's knave. The insult, the desolation and the sorrow give hurt, and she is not as calm as she professes to be.

Such is the speech's purpose for the Proculeius/Dolabella episode. The tragic irony of Antony's last words – 'trust but Proculeius' – is seen in his misjudgement of the two men: Dolabella was the man to trust, not Proculeius; but for the Queen [line 15] 'trusting' is of no avail. Her mind is still with the 'beggar' [16] in relation to the Emperor, rather than with the immediacy of danger. Thus she is easily captured and the philosophy beneath the opening speech falls away in the panic of her tirade. The threats [49–62] are emotionally excessive. From claims to starve, talk and 'wake' herself to death, her imagination encompasses her proposed humiliation in Rome as she is shown in defeat to the common people. Rather than this she imagines better ways to die in her own land, hanging from the Pyramids or lying naked on the mud flats being 'blown' by insects. The word 'blow' here refers to the waterflies laying their eggs over her, although it may also have connotations with the blowing of the wind carrying the smell of her decaying body to her people in the city.

Proculeius as captor ignores such tantrums and terrors, but within the speech Shakespeare has clearly captured an element of the grotesque in Cleopatra's imagination which Plutarch described as a later reality. The historical Cleopatra disfigured herself by tearing her face and body and allowing herself to fall into disease. Shakespeare suggests this degradation through her fancy, but does not stress it since that would detract from his concept of her regality. Her engagement with Proculeius demonstrates Cleopatra's character as it has been throughout the play, imaginative and fiery: moments of calmness and quiet longing erupting into rage or passion. Shakespeare, however, contrasts this element in his creation with a romanticism in the exchange that follows. Neatly he replaces Proculeius with Dolabella. This soldier is to be more sympathetic. His words 'Most noble empress, you have heard of me?' [71] form a significant contrast to Proculeius about whom she had heard, erroneously. Thus Dolabella's introduction places him at a disadvantage. What does it matter whether she has heard of him or not? All she can trust is her own imagination and resolve. Yet paradoxically in its concern the question allows her a moment's pause from the political turmoil to engage her dreams of Antony:

> His legs bestrid the ocean; his reared arm
> Crested the world; his voice was propertied
> As all the tunèd spheres, and that to friends;
> But when he meant to quail and shake the orb,
> He was as rattling thunder. For his bounty,
> There was no winter in't; an Antony it was
> That grew the more by reaping. His delights
> Were dolphin-like; they showed his back above
> The element they lived in. In his livery
> Walked crowns and crownets; realms and islands were
> As plates dropped from his pocket.   [82–92]

Her description is of a Herculean, a giant figure wading the seas and shaping the skies with the arc of his arm, as may be seen in an heraldic emblem. He was as a god whose very voice resembled and contained the harmony of the planets which, according to Pythagoras, made music as they moved in the spheres of heaven. He was tempestuous in command and authority and yet magnanimous, becoming more and more generous as he gave: a man unable to be contained by the world – just as a dolphin cannot be contained within the sea but bursts through the surface showing his back to new elements. He was an Emperor who gave to his attendants lands and kingdoms as if they were silver coins.

Such is Cleopatra's view of her lover and it is one which Shakespeare allows Dolabella to listen to impatiently. Caesar's soldier interjects in an attempt to stem the fantasy, 'Most sovereign creature –', 'Cleopatra –' but there is no sign of a halt until she asks,

> Think you there was or might be such a man
> As this I dreamt of?

– and he replies,

> Gentle madam, no.   [93–4]

To Rome the fantasy that her speech proclaims and the life-style that its imaginative force had created for the couple are spurious and unrealistic. For Dolabella Antony was no god, no Herculean but a great general, now dead. Grief is understandable but pragmatism is required. The only truth now is that Cleopatra will be mocked and degraded.

Thus Shakespeare in the first part of this scene again establishes polarities – realism against imagination – but in their juxtaposition stresses the experience required for their fusion. He prepares Cleopatra for death in relation to her memories and fantasies but also to her present dire circumstances made only too clear by the second phase: the arrival of Caesar.

Phase 2: Caesar and Seleucus

Shakespeare's craftsmanship is seen to the fore in allowing the audience to know of Caesar's dishonourable intentions before he enters. The dramatist requires attention to be focused on the Queen. The Emperor's entrance is proud and his opening question, 'Which is the Queen of Egypt?' [112], may be cruel. Can the Queen, who sailed down the Cydnus as Venus, no longer be recognised? His words [124–33] are silk. There is to be no intimacy with this Emperor, but Cleopatra's reply is aptly feline:

CAES. . . .   I'll take my leave.
CLEO. And may, through all the world; 'tis yours, and we,
       Your scutcheons and your signs of conquest, shall
       Hang in what place you please. . . .   [133–6]

From the earlier reference to the heraldic emblem of the godlike Antony, Shakespeare demonstrates by verbal contrast the reality of defeat as Cleopatra describes herself as a captured shield. Caesar in this scene is abrupt but Cleopatra answers his diffidence by demonstrating her knowledge of the situation. The dramatist, however, introduces a further dimension to the episode through Seleucus.

Often omitted in production, the role of Seleucus, Cleopatra's treasurer, has produced some critical debate as to why Shakespeare included him. The episode is recounted in Plutarch, but not every action within his history is placed in the dramatic text. By introducing the episode, Shakespeare breaks the tension of Caesar and Cleopatra's verbal fencing match, allowing us to see their natures in stark opposition. Ostensibly the Queen is humiliated, but a three-cornered figure of deceit has been established from which a fourth may be discerned. Seleucus deceives Cleopatra who, in the matter of treasure, deceived Caesar, who is in turn attempting to deceive the Queen concerning his plans for her. As Emrys Jones (Penguin edition, p. 278) has demonstrated, Shakespeare is creating a deliberately ambiguous moment based on Plutarch's history. Plutarch shows that Caesar falls into a trap in the sense that, in seeing Cleopatra's deceit over a small matter, he accepts her story that she wished to keep back the money in order to compete on a modest scale with Livia (Caesar's wife) and Octavia. So Plutarch writes:

> Caesar was glad to hear her say so, persuading himself thereby that she had yet a desire to save her life. So he made her answer that he did not only give her that to dispose of at her pleasure which she had kept back, but further promised to use her more honourably and bountifully than she would think for. And so he took his leave of her, supposing he had deceived her. But indeed he was deceived himself.
>
> (*Shakespeare's Plutarch*, p. 289.)

Shakespeare follows his source. Caesar, leaving the stage, assures the Queen:

> Not what you have reserved nor what acknowledged
> Put we i' th' roll of conquest. Still be't yours;
> Bestow it at your pleasure, and believe
> Caesar's no merchant, to make prize with you
> Of things that merchants sold. . . .   [180–4]

As we saw above Cleopatra's remark on his exit –

> He words me, girls, he words me, that I should not
> Be noble to myself. . . .   [191–2]

– illustrates that the Queen is to win the last battle with the Emperor.

The three phases which make the remainder of the scene are conducted almost as a masque of death for Cleopatra. They begin with the images of the Roman and Elizabethan stages [207–21] and her command for her regalia. The death scene itself, however, is preceded by the important comic interlude with the 'rural fellow' [241–78].

Phase 3: Clown

This short episode brings together the images of earth, of death and of sexual activity that have pervaded the play. The force of the exchange revolves around the pun on the word 'die'. It could mean both to decease and to reach a climax of sexual pleasure. Similarly the word 'worm' has a sexual connotation of masculinity, while the word 'lie' refers to lying with someone sexually or deceiving someone. With these placed together with such other words as 'biting', 'pain', 'joy', 'no goodness', 'devil', 'gods', 'dress', 'whoreson', a pattern of sexual ambiguity is established in relation to oncoming death. In this respect the episode comically and grotesquely reflects and comments upon the conduct of the play. Should a woman 'lie' except honestly? In terms of deceit Cleopatra has often lied, and indeed we have just seen a sparring match of lies with Caesar. In terms of sexuality Cleopatra's lying with Antony has led to death. The lovers 'died' in sexuality but now their final 'death', their decease, is with them. The worm is 'an odd worm'. As masculinity it produces the 'joy' of sexual pain. As the snake of the earth it will bring the Queen the joyous finality of life's pain. And what of Cleopatra? Was she 'a dish for the gods' or was she a 'whoreson' dressed by the devil, the strumpet described in the opening scene? Shakespeare with the clown brings the ambiguities, debates, nuances of the play together for the last time before the Queen's death. The clown alienates us, the audience, from the action through his comedy once again placing the issues before us, not in terms of asking for a moral judgement, but as a commentary on the experiences portrayed.

Phase 4: Death

As the clown leaves, Cleopatra turns towards death: 'I have / Immortal longings in me' [279–80]. The phrase is pertinent. Death is to be approached by the Queen as a final sexual act. For the first time in the play she calls Antony, 'Husband'. Through the final experience of sexuality, death itself, she believes that she will find a life freed from the limits of mortality, the bounds of humanity. As being only 'fire' and 'air', relinquishing the 'baser' elements of life (earth and water), Cleopatra in her romanticism can at last have no boundary for her love, as was stated to be the wish of the lovers in the opening scene of the play. She is therefore shown as

prepared for the spirituality of her dreams. But again Shakespeare changes focus slightly as Iras falls dead at her kiss. The
audience's attention is diverted briefly from the Queen only to
return to her in a heightened manner. 'Have I the aspic in my
lips?' [292] she asks. The irony is only too clear since it is her
lips which have led to this moment of death. Softly she quips:

> This proves me base;
> If she first meet the curlèd Antony,
> He'll make demand of her, and spend that kiss
> Which is my heaven to have. . . .   [299–302]

The word 'curlèd' here has the force of conjuring up the beauty
of her dead lover with his curled hair, 'barbered ten times o'er'
[II ii 229] at his first feasting with her. It is the image again of the
classical godhead, and yet one containing the implication of the
curled snake, the asp in the basket, the asp of her lips and at her
breast: the sexuality of the snake which has ruled her history.
The moment of her stage-managed death, with Charmian only
in attendance, sees her again in her royal robes, as Venus, the
eastern star:

CHAR.   O eastern star!
CLEO.   Peace, peace!
       Dost thou not see my baby at my breast,
       That sucks the nurse asleep?
CHAR.   O, break! O, break!
CLEO. As sweet as balm, as soft as air, as gentle –
       O, Antony! Nay I will take thee too.
                              (*She applies another asp to her arm*)
       What should I stay –   (*She dies*)
CHAR. In this vile world? . . .   [307–13]

It is certainly a moment of 'theatrical sublimity', but throughout the scene Shakespeare has prepared for it through recount-
ing the parodoxes, ambiguities and deceits of the play as a
whole. The moment of sublimity is therefore tempered by the
consistent alienating commentary demonstrated through the
exchanges with Proculeius, Dolabella, Caesar, Seleucus and
the Clown. Thus the final experience is not one portrayed as
Cleopatra's imaginative fantasy but rather as her dream fused
with the stark reality of death.

Phase 5: Epilogue

The dramatist concludes with an epilogue in which Caesar enters the room where the dead Queen of Love sits 'marble constant' on her throne. The romanticism is reduced as he inquiringly discovers how she died, gives order for her solemn funeral, and for the return to Rome. He mentions fame, glory and pity but in his realisation of the inevitable is practical. Thus Shakespeare leaves the play with the romantic and the expedient, the imaginative and the pragmatic: a final image of the complex experience of life and love which he has created throughout.

PART TWO: PERFORMANCE

6 INTRODUCTION

We do not know in which theatre *Antony and Cleopatra* was performed during Shakespeare's day. As mentioned earlier, it may have been either *The Globe* before 2500 to 3000 people, or at the much smaller *Blackfriars* theatre, holding about 400. Either way, the part of Cleopatra would have been taken by a boy actor, as would the roles of Iras, Charmian and Octavia. Even if presented at *The Globe*, the play's impact would not have lacked immediacy, even intimacy; such was the design of the theatre that no member of the audience would have been more than twenty-five feet from the action.

The manner of acting would have been more stylised than the one we are accustomed to in popular theatre or on television today. The texts of many Elizabethan plays demonstrate, particularly in their employment of chorus characters such as Enobarbus, a tendency towards mannerist commentary, where one character draws attention to aspects of the play or appeals to members of the audience to use their imagination – 'Piece out our imperfections with your thoughts' [*Henry V*, Prologue 23]. Enobarbus's set speech, 'The barge she sat in . . .', is a prime example of this technique; it aims to conjure up for the audience the atmosphere of Egyptian grandeur and the resplendent beauty of Cleopatra. Although certain props and costumes would have been employed, and music used, the imaginative setting of the play depended largely on the language.

As such, *Antony and Cleopatra* does not lend itself to realistic acting. There are no great love scenes in this drama of love and power politics. Embraces, kisses, romance – these are reported on; but what we see between the couple on stage is frustration, argument, reconciliation. Similarly, there is no call by Shakes-

peare for moments of great spectacle – although, in the
nineteenth century, producers vied with one another in their
visual extravaganzas of the play. *Antony and Cleopatra* depends
on no such conceptions. Rather, like Elizabethan plays in
general, it gains its power through implication. Our imagination is appealed to mainly through the ear, not the eye; hence
Shakespeare's play can frustrate a modern audience's expecta-
tion, fostered by the visual media of television and film.
Further, the predominant mid-twentieth-century acting styles
in the popular media and in the conventional realistic schools
of theatre seem to have found the play difficult. For nearly
twenty years (1953–72) *Antony and Cleopatra* was not staged at
Stratford, but during the seventies and eighties it has become
more accessible in the theatre, possibly because its interpretation as a political or an intimate play, or both, is gradually
being fostered. The influence of Bertolt Brecht on modern
theatre has demonstrated that 'epic' does not necessarily
equate with splendour and spectacle as in a Hollywood movie.
Nevertheless, past traditions and popular expectations also
influence directors; and thus, in the past thirty years, only one
director, Peter Brook, has shown the diverse thinking
towards the play which the text often demands in relation to
convention. This he did in a production mounted at Stratford
in 1978. Even then, however, working in an artistic vacuum,
Brook only managed, as we shall see, to lay the foundations for
a stage re-evaluation of the work. His production interested
many commentators, but did not convince them that it was of
major significance.

Of other post-war productions a number have attempted to
set the drama as a contrast with other plays on a similar
subject: in 1951 Michael Benthall directed Vivien Leigh and
Laurence Olivier in the play in tandem with Shaw's *Caesar and
Cleopatra*; in 1972 Richard Johnson and Janet Suzman played
the roles in the context of Trevor Nunn's Roman season at
Stratford, in repertory with *Julius Caesar, Coriolanus* and *Titus
Andronicus*; in 1977 the Prospect Theatre Company staged the
drama in contrast with Dryden's *All for Love*; in 1981 Jonathan
Miller presented the play as part of the BBC's complete
Shakespeare series. All these productions were of interest, and
three of them – Benthall/Olivier (1951), Nunn (1972) and

Miller (1980) – will form, with Peter Brook's (1978), the focus of the present discussion.

One other production, however, needs to receive more than passing mention. In 1973 Tony Richardson staged an experimental interpretation at the Bankside Globe. Vanessa Redgrave and Julian Glover took the lead parts in a performance that insisted on the political relevance of the work. The production went totally against traditional readings of the text, with Vanessa Redgrave as 'a decadent imperialist in a red wig, orange sunglasses and white pants suit' reeling 'drunkenly on three-inch heels', throwing 'coke bottles at flunkeys' and shouting 'raucously at her drably dressed maids'. Julian Glover complemented the scene as 'a dandyish, cigar-smoking subaltern in khakis – and so narcissistic that when his Eros killed himself, Antony fell down' (Margaret Lamb, *'Antony and Cleopatra' on the English Stage*, p. 107). Such productions are instructive if only in forcing us back to the text and to other performances in order to find their artistic appropriateness.

7 DESIGN

One of the first problems a director has to overcome in staging a play is that of set design. However much he might like to allow his set to evolve from his rehearsals, practicality demands that major decisions concerning the construction, or non-construction, of the set have to be made early. Such decisions naturally impose artistic limitations on the company and its interpretations of the drama.

Benthall/Olivier Production, London and New York, 1951

For Michael Benthall, directing the Oliviers at the St James's Theatre in London, and later at the Ziegfeld in New York, the set for *Antony and Cleopatra* was to have a major feature in common with *Caesar and Cleopatra*. In Act I of Shaw's play,

Julius Caesar finds the young Cleopatra sleeping between the 'great paws' of a Sphinx. In presenting the two plays on alternate nights, Benthall used this motif as a unifying element. Fittingly, it was to reappear in Shakespeare's play as the entrance to Cleopatra's monument. The Queen leaned from between the paws, Charmian next to her leaning on one of its legs, Iras on the other, to raise the dying Antony. A symmetrical pattern was established defining to some extent the interpretation of the play: where Julius Caesar found the Queen, Mark Antony lost her in his death.

Antony and Cleopatra has become notorious for its scene-changes. In the spectacular nineteenth-century productions scene-changes took so long as sometimes to account for 'one-third of the evening' (see Lamb, pp. 72–98). The play was also repatterned in order to simplify it according to the neo-classical unities. Although such measures are not the answer for modern productions, the many short and swift episodes – moving from Alexandria to Rome to Athens and back – have consistently presented problems to designers and directors, especially of the realistic school. Benthall's answer at the St James's theatre was to employ a revolving stage designed by Roger Furse. Rome on the one side was depicted as a functional city with sturdy Italian columns in cold marble. The set revolved and presented a warmer Egypt with slender artistic Corinthian colonnades attached by cornices. Drapes could be hung from these, again to give the impression of a more luxurious world. As the sets revolved characters would walk off and onto stage allowing a unity to develop through contrast and correspondence. Behind all was a cyclorama which showed the shadows of the moving stage – pillars, steps and characters – giving the impression of constant movement and fluidity.

In costume the contrast of the two worlds was maintained: Rome in efficient, military cobalt; Egypt in the bright colours of the gods, scarlet and gold. Cleopatra's court was one of luxury, with her soldiers and male attendants in loin cloths, their bronze bodies as if open to the sun: luxuriousness signified merely by their copper wristlets. Great fans of black, blue, yellow and gold aided the total effect, an impression of warmth dominated by the Queen and Emperor. Antony wore a slit

tunic of gold and scarlet cloth, his body, like the Egyptian
soldiers, bronzed and off-setting his golden hair flecked with
the hint of grey. Cleopatra wore heavy red lipstick and nail
polish. Her eyes were darkened by mascara and shadow. In a
long-sleeved chiffon dress with laced bodice, she exuded luxury
and beauty. Her crown was blue-flamed with golden lengths
draped below her ears and complementing her golden
bracelets. Yet, as with the grey in Antony's hair, in this touch of
blue and gold there was the hint of cold beneath the warmth of
splendour. Even in the Egyptian heat, the chill of luxury – in
age and decadence – though warmer than the ice of Roman
efficiency, naturally declined to the bareness of the mausoleum.
For the final scene the Sphinx revolved to expose a cold empty
interior with just three ionic pillars and Cleopatra's low-backed
throne. The symmetry of the production was maintained to the
last. Cleopatra was now as the Sphinx. She died head erect,
eyes closed, blended into the marble of death itself, while at
each foot the soldiers found one of her companions, Iras and
Charmian. Her robe depicted the flames of death, while her
coronet displayed over her brow a small phallic decoration – at
once important and yet insignificant.

In design this production was clearly intellectual and
practical in pushing its point from Shaw to Shakespeare and
back again, but it was still within the romantic tradition of the
play visually emphasising Cleopatra's beauty and Antony's
heroism. The mechanical innovation, for London, of the
revolving set relieved to some extent the problems of scenic
design, which at the turn of the century had bedevilled Sir
Frank Benson whose set in total weighed twenty tons. But in its
mechanism it began a new era of difficulty for the play which
was demonstrated more significantly in Trevor Nunn's 1972
production at Stratford-upon-Avon.

Trevor Nunn's Production, RSC, Stratford, 1972

As did the 1951 Benthall/Olivier production, Nunn's of 1972
sought to convey stark differences between the Roman and
Egyptian courts through contrasts in colour. Octavius Caesar's
cold palace was dominated by the severity of black and white

and the strictly utilitarian furniture. To the rear was a white sky or a huge map of the Empire.* There were touches only of officious imperial purple to ease the eye since even the conference table was in off-white 'textured stone'. Egypt, in contrast, was resplendent in multi-coloured hangings, furniture and costume. There was a huge silken canopy held by golden slaves befitting the luxurious dignity of the Queen; divans and cushions littered the stage and servants held large fans. Gold was the dominant colour, contrasted with orange and deep blue. The court lounged in amicable languid conversation, the many eunuchs giving the whole an impression of comfortable but controlled decadence beneath the warm sky. Gold masks and elaborate crowns were worn and musicians held ornately-designed instruments fitting for an ancient Egyptian court. When Cleopatra came to meet Antony after his victory she did so to the accompaniment of tinkling bells, like a frivolous goddess detached from reality. Such an interpretation was textually sound and worked within the theatrical traditions of the play. The distraction, however, if such it was, came from the set itself. For the Roman season new hydraulics had been installed under the Stratford stage, allowing the floor to rise and change shape in a mechanical extravaganza of technical power. A flick of a switch, it seemed, would slowly transform a flat open space in an off-white box into a set of steps, a pyramid, monument (exterior or interior), a Roman conference room or a galleon complete with mast. The transformations were geometrically dazzling but they detracted from the play, halting rather than aiding its narrative or thematic flow. The pyramid shape was splendid but its height limited, Pompey's galleon was detailed but mechanical, and thus judgement and appreciation were in danger of focusing on the attempts at technological realism rather than on the play. This was unfortunate since the acting was good and the interpretation and characterisation consistent. When later the production was televised it seemed to enjoy more success than it did at Stratford, although in 1972 it was the best of the four Roman productions.

---

*See stage-set, plate 4.

Jonathan Miller's Production, BBC Television, 1980

Television, however, presents its own problems. Shakespeare's theatre has little in common with the demands of transmission or with a family audience sitting in a living room rather than standing around a thrust-stage. With the notable exception of *All's Well That Ends Well*, the BBC Shakespeare series has found great difficulty in conveying the range of a Shakespearean play through the mass medium. *All's Well* succeeded perhaps because it is an intimate play. Many of the camera shots were taken to give the impression of the intimacy of theme: small rooms, pleasantly projected in corridors; shadows and shades and Vermeer-like lighting and setting seemed to encompass the play. *Antony and Cleopatra*, it can be well argued, is also an intimate play but one set in the expanse of Empire. The decision between the intimacy and the expanse is one that directors have to take – and convention, as we have seen, usually opts for the latter. For television, however, the former does present a strong case but one which the BBC perhaps did not wish to take. The policy of the series throughout has been for 'safe' productions and interpretations. The result with the 1980 production of *Antony and Cleopatra* was a fall between two stools. Jonathan Miller, in deciding on an expansive production, wished to employ the vast facilities of the film studio at Ealing. This proved unavailable for rehearsal purposes and therefore for the production. The result was that the play was mounted in the more cramped BBC television studios. The production nevertheless proved challenging in Miller's concept of the play and the way it can be presented to a modern audience within the limitations set him by the Corporation:

> . . . my first problem was to discover some image which reconciled the images of three periods – the period of the audience, the period of the writer, and the period to which he nominally referred in the text. . . . If you have a text which is written in sixteenth-century English and you present it in a classical Rome or a classical antiquity with which Shakespeare himself was unacquainted, it simply doesn't marry; you get a curious amalgam. I had to find some image which would reconcile these conflicts.
>
> (BBC, *'Antony and Cleopatra': The Production*, pp. 17–18.)

The result came from his own enthusiasm for Baroque art. He chose the style of Veronese (c. 1528–88) and in particular the painting *The Family of Darius at the feet of Alexander*, which he saw as a 'reconciling image . . . created by a sixteenth-century imagination into which are fed the images of the classical past, but altered and dissolved and finally crystallised in that imagination'. The characters were draped in warm Italian folds and colours: yellow, gold, orange, red and silver. The dresses were full and long with tunics, capes, frills and lace. Neck lines were open and sleek, jewellery rich and tasteful. Antony was richly clothed in a silk folded shirt of red and silver, with a multi-coloured garment draped over one shoulder. The court was full of golden cloths and drapes, of coloured seating and cushions. There was plentiful fruit and even a tame monkey straight from a Baroque painting, and there was the contrast of light. Bright white light from outside a large entrance emphasised the coolness of the interior in shadow. Later the scenes took place in tents. There the impression was still of cushions, cloths and folds – but also of the heat, only just being kept, like Caesar, at bay. In contrast, Octavius's court and tent were again characterised by military authority demonstrable in costumes of dark blue and green and a plethora of maps and documents. The music by Stephen Oliver was also baroque in style so that the total impression was sixteenth- and seventeenth-century Venetian rather than Shakespearean or Egyptian. There was too much refinement and good taste for the characterisation that Shakespeare gives his play. Because of the nineteen-inch screen the focus was not on Shakespeare's vast Veronese canvas, as Bradley described it, but on the detail of the folds, the silks and the colour; and therefore the required effect naturally fell short.

Peter Brook's Production, RSC, Stratford, 1978

Sally Jacobs's setting for Peter Brook's 1978 production was revolutionary in moving away from spectacle and splendour altogether. The emphasis of the play was to be on its intimacy. But Brook suffered Miller's problem in reverse. The design of the Royal Shakespeare Theatre is such that members of the audience can be tens of yards away from the action. In such a theatre small-scale productions are almost impossible, as has been frequently discovered by directors coming to work in it from the RSC studio theatre, The Other Place. Nevertheless, Brook bravely dispensed with pomp. Sally Jacobs's set had four translucent, bronzed screens semi-circled across the upper centre of the stage. In front of each there was a bench, and in front of each bench a square piece of matting. Within the screens was the personal world of the courts and of the protagonists' relationship; beyond was the turbulent world of politics and war. The battles were denoted by blood being splattered on the screens from behind. There were no thrones, no divans, no luxury – merely the plain wooden forms, two gilded stools and a few cushions. It was Brook's 'empty space' in which he would depict the simplicity of a complex affair. Even the monument was symbolised by a plain red carpet suspended above the acting areas while Cleopatra and her attendants ran beneath, so as to allow it to fall to the floor and assume its simple function. Antony was consequently pulled along the floor to the monument by three long pieces of cloth wrapped around his body and held by the three women.* Without the encumbrance of luxury, splendour and frills, Brook's attention was on the words spoken and the relationship created between the lovers. Within the empty space was the cajoling, arguing and ferocious intimacy of a couple who had shut out the politics of the world so as to deal with each other in the most intense of manners.

8   CLEOPATRA

From the sets the varying interpretations of the play can be discerned, but the centrality of the production lies with the lovers themselves. The four Cleopatras we are considering – Vivien Leigh in 1951, Janet Suzman in 1972, Glenda Jackson in

---

*See group in plate 5.

1978, and Jane Lapotaire in 1980 – form interesting contrasts. The historical Cleopatra was not outstandingly good-looking, although the world's imaginative concept of her is one of great physical beauty. Shakespeare's Cleopatra, as we have seen, was a boy speaking the words and playing the role of a neo-goddess. The strength of the part lies in characterisation and presence, although there should be no objections if this is fused with beauty.

When Dame Edith Evans played the role for the second time in 1946 at the Piccadilly Theatre – she had played it previously in 1925 at the Old Vic – one unkind critic saw a resemblance throughout to Queen Victoria. However, a distinguished reviewer, W. A. Darlington, thought it to be the best revival of the play he had ever seen. Certainly Dame Edith brought a presence that allowed her to break conventions and provide power and originality. She even defied expectations by return-ing, in both 1925 and 1946, to the Jacobean staging, more textually accurate, of dying not on a throne but a day-bed or stately couch. In 1946 this was placed just left of stage-centre. In 1952 Peggy Ashcroft, playing opposite Michael Redgrave in a greatly praised production at Stratford, gave the role a lasciviousness and confidence which came from the poetic power of the text rather than from any external interpretation or imposed reading. In 1969 Margaret Leighton at the Chichester Festival theatre displayed vitality in the splendour of her regality and the memory of her sensuality – although some critics felt that her immediate dealings with Antony, John Clements, were cool in comparison with her general approach to the part. The interesting note with all these Cleopatras is that it was the power of interpretation and presence of the actress, rather than her beauty, which gave credence and success to the role.

Vivien Leigh: Benthall/Olivier Production, 1951

With Vivien Leigh the case was a little different. She was particularly attractive and her beauty consequently dominated the interpretation. When she was imprisoned in her monu-ment, Roman soldiers came onto the scene to peer through the

2. Two contrasting Cleopatras: the beautiful Vivien Leigh, *Benthall/Olivier Production*, 1951 (Photograph © Angus McBean) (inset), and the sensually intense Helen Mirren, *Adrian Noble Production*, 1982 (Photograph © Joe Cocks).

3. *Trevor Nunn Production, 1972.* Act III sc. xiii. Even in fights with Antony (Richard Johnson), Janet Suzman displayed a powerful sensuality. Photograph © Reg Wilson.

4. *Trevor Nunn Production, 1972.* Act II sc. ii. Agrippa (Desmond Stokes) proposes Antony's marriage to Octavia. Note the austerity of Rome. Octavius (Corin Redgrave), Lepidus (Raymond Westwell) and Antony (Richard Johnson) are seated at the conference table. Enobarbus (Patrick Stewart) leans on Antony's chair. Photograph © Joe Cocks.

5. *Peter Brook Production, 1978.* Act IV sc. xv. Charmian (Paola Dionisotti), Cleopatra (Glenda Jackson) and Iras (Juliet Stevenson) 'heave aloft' Antony (Alan Howard) by pulling him along the floor to their carpet. Photograph © Joe Cocks.

6. *Jonathan Miller TV Production, 1980.* Act IV sc. xv. The dying Antony (Colin Blakely) is brought to Cleopatra (Jane Lapotaire) at the monument. BBC copyright photograph.

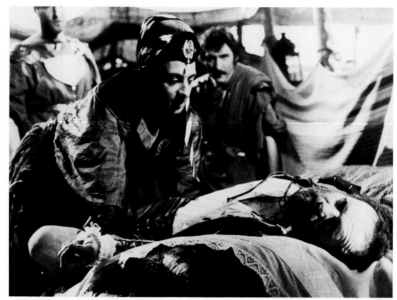

7. *Jonathan Miller TV Production, 1980*. Act IV sc. xiv. Alexas (Darien Anghadi) informs Antony (Colin Blakely) that Cleopatra is in the monument. BBC copyright photograph.

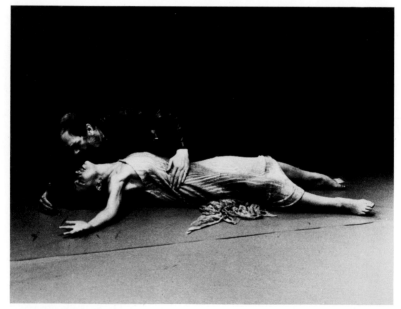

8. *Adrian Noble Production, 1982*. Act III sc. xiii. Another interpretation of the sensuality of argument: Antony (Michael Gambon), Cleopatra (Helen Mirren). Compare with the 1972 Johnson/Suzman interpretation. Photograph © Times Newspapers Ltd.

bars at the creation, 'enforcing Cleopatra's speech about how she will be exhibited in Rome' (Alice Venezky, *Shakespeare Quarterly*, 3, 1952, p. 123). The exhibition, however, was to be in the monument itself. In the last scene, with long auburn hair, exotic eastern make-up and jewellery, she assumed the mythic appearance of the Queen of the Nile. It was the climax of her interpretation. Vivien Leigh's role, enhanced by her richly modulated, low-pitched voice, was one purging the carnality of her love through the movement towards death.

She seemed to neglect, however, the elements so intrinsically part of the Queen's sexuality. Reviewers noted that she was soft and enchanting but neither royal nor sensual, and that she lacked the basic temperament and range for the role. Her success lay with the externals, the beauty, the costume, the mystical appearance* which found its greatest success in the iconic vision of death. One critic, Tynan, went too far in his attack, becoming personally insulting. Others more reasonably saw her portrayal as attractive but inaccurate in a production which achieved no mean acclaim. George Rylands is representative:

> Who will forget Vivien Leigh, robed and crowned in the habiliments of an Egyptian goddess, beauty on a monument smiling extremity out of act? The gipsy, the ribaudred nag, the boggler, the triple turn'd whore, the fragment on Cneius Pompey's trencher, were all forgotten. There never was such a person any way. The *femme fatale* of 'the Romantic Agony', the Cleopatra of Gautier and Flaubert still exerts her spell and Shakespeare's boy player is suppressed.
>
> (*Shakespeare Survey*, 6, 1953, pp. 141–2.)

Janet Suzman: Trevor Nunn's Production, 1972

Miss Suzman was also a highly attractive Cleopatra, but in a very different manner from Vivien Leigh. She played the part almost as an Amazon queen, although one breast was not severed. On the contrary, her physicality was overtly empha-

---

*See plate 1.

sised in a portrayal that was richly feminine and yet simultaneously masculine. There was a determination to gain her desire
and defend her actions. With breasts emphasised, she still
displayed a manliness in her stance, her walk and her
conference. She would sit legs apart or stride across the stage.
In battle dress she looked formidable, sword at her side, her
metallic skirt glittering in the light. As critics noted, she was
athletic rather than sensual but nevertheless highly attractive.
She was a woman deep in love, but she was also a queen, and an
enigma.*

Thus her range was admirable, moving from regality to
playfulness to childishness to pitiful defeat to final dignity.
After the defeat at Actium, momentarily she drew back on
seeing Antony in despair. Yet earlier, in her thoughts of the
Emperor, she was languid, dreaming and sensual. Lying on a
couch for 'Give me to drink mandragora', she conveyed the
impression of hours of love spent with her warrior. Nevertheless, there was a calculation in her relationship with him. In an
excellent review (*New Statesman*, 25 Aug. 1972), Benedict
Nightingale recalls the way she displayed an ironic tone on
'Can Fulvia *die?*' and how she demonstrated a contempt for the
departing Antony on 'smooth success be strewed before your
feet'. This detachment aided the ambiguity. To what extent did
she love her Antony? To what extent was she merely infatuated
by power? As Caesar entered the monument, she crawled
centre-stage, bowing low to him. As he gave her his hand, she
looked at it inquiringly: was this man as great as her Antony?
The strength of the portrayal was that Suzman was consistently
the enigma. Her hair was raven black, her skin tawny,
outwardly denoting her experience. For Antony such a woman
frustrated and enraptured. She seemed the equivalent to the
youth he had lost, so that her playfulness was magnetic. Her
jest with the salted fish was recounted with humorous cred-
ulity, and yet she was deeply serious about her relationship and
the conduct of the war. Her affair was therefore public rather
than intimate since it ruled the world. Consequently, her
moods, perfectly matched by variation in the voice, constantly
changed between the two aspects leaving him literally breath-

*See plate 3.

less for a response. He could believe that she could send her navy to victory, but was equally led to fly after her at Actium.

In this respect Suzman seemed to capture Shakespeare's complexity of character in its fullest sense. Where her dream of Antony was recounted, it was done with the vitality that had pervaded the play; as the woman who could 'Hop forty paces through the public street; / And, having lost her breath, she spoke, and panted, / That she did make defect perfection' [II ii 234–6]. Thus the dream was not of Antony so much as an expression of her character. She had enjoyed her love in sensuality, in war and in politics, and had attempted to match him in each area. Her outrage with the messenger, however, was not as credible as in other productions since her conception of the role was more calculated than tempestuous. Such an interpretation led to an unemotional though awed effect in her death scene. This was the final calculation. Her eyes glazed and the lights dimmed again on an iconic vision but one which was the culmination of an intelligent and artistic approach to this complex role.

Glenda Jackson: Peter Brook's Production, 1978

If Suzman was aware of the public nature of Cleopatra's love, Glenda Jackson in the next Stratford production was concerned with the personal relationship. No two readings, it seems, could be so far apart, and yet both proved equally valid: a statement which attests the depth of the play. In contrast to convention, Miss Jackson wore what could be irreverently described as a candy-striped sackcloth. In clothes there was no gaudy majesty, pomp or beauty. Her hair was close-cropped, her face and arms unadorned by jewellery or fashion. Jackson's Cleopatra was not to be a sex object ensnaring Antony by her looks, but a Queen who did not need the accoutrements of pomp or sensuality to establish her character and authority. In a *Guardian* interview (2 July 1979) she stated:

> Queens aren't queens because of the clothes they wear. It's as much the way others on the stage react to you as the way you look . . . there is always the sense that she could if she wanted, say, 'I'm

going to kill you', or, 'I'm going to have you killed'. It's this sense of somebody really holding the power of life and death over people that gives her an autocratic life.

Her regality was an inner confidence which allowed her to dispense with pomp and so concentrate on her relationship with Antony. For the audience this was seen in the conduct of the opening exchange. On her taunt, 'that blood of thine / Is Caesar's homager', she asserted her authority by moving past him so as to sit on a cushion centre-right of stage, where she remained, forcing him to pace agitatedly and guiltily about the stage. Antony had to move to her, kneel by her and coax her from her mood on 'What sport tonight?', lifting her to her feet on 'Come, my queen'. In this way Brook established the centrality of Jackson's role through controlled movement and attention to character. This was to be a Cleopatra who ruled by authority.

When in a rage, therefore, all about her trembled. No more was this so than when the messenger brought the news of Antony's marriage [II v]. The messenger entered to her downstage-centre, where he knelt. Charmian was just behind her, Mardian, Iras and Alexas to stage-right centre and upper. He delivered his tale which Cleopatra received with some condescension, tickling him under the chin on 'Th' art an honest man'. As she became more irritated with his nervousness and circumlocution, she moved away from him and sat on a stool downstage-right. With the messenger still kneeling downstage-centre, there was consequently a distance between them for the revelation of the marriage. The line 'For the best turn o'th'bed' caused initial movement, not from the Queen, but from Charmian. As the messenger confirmed his story Cleopatra exploded, crossing from her stool to grab him by the hair. Charmian in her concern moved downstage-right, where she knelt looking towards, and thus focusing attention on, the two characters centre-stage. The scene accelerated. Cleopatra kicked the messenger, dragged him about the stage by the hair, shaking him in her rage. All quaked, Iras and Alexas retreating towards the wings and Mardian pressing himself back against one of the translucent screens. At last, on 'Rogue, thou hast lived too long', Cleopatra drew a knife from the folds of the messenger's own clothes. It was time for him to leave. He ran up the left of the stage between the two screens and across the rear to escape right. She followed him to the left screens and then looped back to centre-left. It was near-chaos for the Queen's companions. Alexas went in search of the messenger while Cleopatra threw the knife after him, angrily circling on the spot. Mardian in fear was looking to and from the wings while Iras followed Alexas out, returning to whisper something to Charmian. She then reported 'He is afeared to come'. When the messenger did return matters cooled slightly. The Queen pressed his head close to her in despair before pacing up and down the stage in her frustration. The messenger's mind, however, was firmly on retreat and escape. He inched his way to the left, bowing to the Queen as he did so, to make a relieved exit on 'Lie they upon thy hand, / And be undone by 'em'. The mood now changed again. As Cleopatra reflected on her 'dispraise' of Caesar, Charmian crossed to her. The Queen fell to her knees on 'I faint', but shook Charmian and Iras from her as they tried to help. Alexas knelt to receive instructions and then Cleopatra, attended by her two women sadly, wearily moved downstage-centre. With the words, 'Let him for ever go – let him not, Charmian', she hugged her companion. There was no panic now but intense compassion. Mardian fell to his knees and bowed low for his instruction, and then ran off while, with her women, Cleopatra made her exit downstage-right.

The episode was Glenda Jackson at her best. There was uneasy humour followed by storms; pathos and sadness in the very frustration of her love; but throughout there was also her regal power, shown in the attitude of her court. When the Queen stormed, everyone moved. The scene characterised Miss Jackson as a Cleopatra at once stable and yet quickly changeable in mood; sometimes sad, sometimes languid, sometimes tempestuous but always striving, acting a role to bring a contentment. It was this element of role-play, a knowledge of authority but a realisation that this could not bring her peace, that allowed the intimacy of her love at moments of remorse. This was depicted through an intelligent stage realisation of the text in the scene following Antony's defeat at sea which counterpointed her episode of rage.

At the conclusion of Antony's speech [III xi 1–24], Iras and Charmian almost forced her on stage, supporting her as they led her around the back of the screens to enter up right. The weeping Antony was kneeling diagonally opposite her just to the right of the stage-left screen. As she saw him she attempted to escape but was prevented by her women. Eros, who had entered opposite Cleopatra, coming towards her, now crossed to the Emperor, making the spatial link between the protagonists. The Queen on 'O, Juno!' collapsed to the floor. Iras and Charmian tried to revive her, while Eros attempted to coax the Emperor. As Antony talked of Cassius and Brutus, Cleopatra, still upstage, was gently helped to her feet by the women. Supported by them, she moved towards Antony as Eros forced the kneeling Emperor to look at her. As Antony chided, Charmian gradually released the Queen, who knelt to the right of him. Their task completed Eros, Iras and Charmian moved away upstage where the ladies then knelt. In Antony's following profession of love, Cleopatra collapsed in tears – 'O, my pardon!' – until, on 'Give me a kiss', they embraced, rising on 'Love, I am full of lead' to walk slowly down centre-stage and then off stage-left. Here was the intimacy of their affair, but it was one controlled, not only by Glenda Jackson, Alan Howard and Peter Brook, but by the dramatist. The staging of the scene evolved directly from the Shakespearean text. The director and actors required few accoutrements and no extraneous material since they trusted the text. There they found that Shakespeare had indicated the kind of action and even the moves required to gain the theatricality of a scene such as III xi, and consequently of the play as a whole.

It was true, as some reviewers noted with regret, that Glenda Jackson did not present the Cleopatra of Enobarbus's barge speech. This was left to our imagination as we listened to the text. Some, however, may have justifiably felt that the visual portrayal was so stark as blatantly to contradict the poetry. The point is debatable. Certainly, the production did not emphasise the neo-deity of the Queen – which, as we saw above, is a valid line to take – yet neither did it forget that Cleopatra was first created for a boy actor. The Queen's sexuality was private in her relationship with Antony, although renowned throughout the world. She was an Elizabeth I in a very different and much hotter climate: powerful, but wary of her own feelings and emotions.

To some extent this presented problems, particularly in the last act. Here her hyperbolic dreams of Antony were too romantic, and consequently incongruous with the woman we had hitherto seen. Although, like Janet Suzman's, Glenda Jackson's portrayal of the death scene lacked emotional effect, it did so from the very different perspective depicted throughout: the presentation to the world and herself of a suspicion of love and emotion rather than a calculation of it for personal or political ends. In this regard, Peter Brook preceded the episode with a highly stylised piece of comedy. The rural fellow was a true clown with a red nose who ended up with his shoes on his hands as he explained the nature of the asp to the Queen. It was a detailed piece of comedy, alienating in direction, so that the Queen's death might be understood in the context of her authority and of an objective presentation of the role. Miss Jackson's Cleopatra could never live in the same world as Octavius Caesar. She had suffered a defeat, personal and political, with the death of Antony, so that the essence of her authority was in danger. Brook also emphasised this by including the Seleucus scene, not as an episode of deception, but as one emphasising her defeat. The only power left to Cleopatra was that over herself. Thus her death was in keeping with the portrayal of her. It was the final remnant of her authority rather than a moment of great emotion, and one once again conducted with detailed symmetry. After closing the Queen's eyes, Charmian painted the lids and adjusted the crown before applying the asp to her own bosom. She then fell at right angles downstage-left of the throne, parallel in death with the body of Iras, creating a final patterned image.

Jane Lapotaire: Jonathan Miller's Television Production, 1980

To play Cleopatra for television demands a new look at the role in relation to the restrictions that the medium imposes. Television does not allow for immediate audience response which in the theatre forms the atmosphere and encourages the creativity of the artists. That level of stimulus in mass applause, attentiveness, silence and encouragement is something towards which Shakespeare directed his plays. For the actress, the changing reaction of the audience (for example, in Peter Brook's production, from laughter at the clown to a quiet attentiveness in the preparation for death) stimulates her performance. The actress knows that she has the audience at her command, and the adrenalin flows that little bit quicker. There is also the matter of language. The screen does not seem to be in harmony with the rhetoric of sixteenth- and seventeenth-century poetry. Producers and directors have attempted to reduce the incongruity in all manner of ways – realistic settings, voice-over techniques, script rewriting, imitation Elizabethan settings – but in the end have come to no satisfactory solution. Nevertheless, a guiding principle has tended to be a reduction of the rhetorical quality of the verse, making it more prosaic. There is something false about this, but equally there is something false about Shakespeare on television itself. It would, of course, be a cultural crime for our greatest dramas not to be produced before the widest audience possible, and yet the problems are still formidable.

In coping with them, Jane Lapotaire recounts that she constantly had to force herself to think 'naturalistically' rather than 'stylistically' in the delivery of her lines. Her Cleopatra has therefore to be regarded in the light of this basic incongruity of the medium with the text. As such it proved to be a challenging portrayal. Her Cleopatra is not beautiful in the sense of Vivien Leigh or Elizabeth Taylor, but she is attractive, lively and intelligent, as the text demands. In this respect, Miss Lapotaire plays the role as one of great vitality at the beginning of the work. She teases Antony, jesting with him as if trying to find the real man beneath. In the search is the romance, but in the discovery is the disillusionment not so much with Antony himself as with the impossibility of her dream. As the play progresses Lapotaire's Cleopatra becomes quieter, sadder and more reflective. This can be seen by a look at two scenes.

In Act I scene ii, Miller keeps her in vision during the banter of Charmian, Iras, Alexas and the Soothsayer. Charmian and the Soothsayer are kept centre-picture, with Iras to the right complete with monkey and phallic hairstyle, and Alexas to the left. Between Charmian and the Soothsayer in deep focus

Antony can be seen caressing Cleopatra as they both half-attentively listen to the fun. The point is clear: the caressing is as superficial and light as the comedy. But when the Soothsayer touches on a matter of life and death – 'You shall outlive the lady whom you serve' – the tone begins to change. Cleopatra's attention momentarily concentrates on the debate, while Enobarbus, unknown to her, whispers in Antony's ear and leads him away to hear the messengers. As the banter continues, Cleopatra realises her lover is missing. She looks around, fidgets and grows more and more impatient, until she breaks up the group on 'Saw you my lord?' It is an episode of realisation that the caresses cannot be permanent and that the world holds its authority still. Her problem is to reconcile her dream of love with the realities that its conduct must bring.

By Act III scene xi, the fact of her romantic disillusionment has established itself in a pertinent way. Much of this scene is cut by the director in order to take the emphasis off Antony's self-recrimination in relation to the past, so as to emphasise visually the immediacy of defeat and Cleopatra's reaction to it. Antony's lines about Philippi are omitted, as is much of his opening speech dwelling on the instructions to his soldiers for their safe escape and the shame of cowardice at his age. Here the poetic image of the mutiny of his hairs, white against brown, is sacrificed for the close-up of his tensed face and shots of Cleopatra's hesitancy and concern. Of similar importance is the omission of Cleopatra's lines 'Let me sit down, O, Juno!', and the lines through which Charmian, Iras and Eros show their insistence in attempting to bring the lovers together – 'See you here, sir?', 'Madam!', 'Madam, O good empress!', 'Sir, sir!'. These lines are implicit stage directions. In Brook's production, as we have seen, Cleopatra's need to sit down results in her collapsing to the floor in her distraction. In Miller's television version, the omission of such lines allows the director to make the Shakespearean point through the visual image. The focus is placed on Antony at the front of the screen and Cleopatra tentatively, hand slightly outstretched, approaching from the rear. The camera thereby concentrates our vision on the general's taut face and tensed hands clasped together at his knees and the Queen's uncertain, worried movement. The visual image communicates Cleopatra's anxiety to such an extent that she hardly needs the verbal encouragement of her companions. Instead, their support is signified by Miss Lapotaire's glancing back towards them at the entrance to the tent. We see a concerned and saddened Queen, devoid of romantic exuberance but full of a maturer love for her Antony. There seems to be an unselfishness about her as she kneels by him, looking into his face, her voice temporarily breaking on 'O, my pardon!', and her lips gently kissing his hand on 'Give me a kiss'. Her repentance is consequently a matter, not of humiliation, but of revelation – both to Cleopatra and the audience. Through the visual blocking of the scene she conveys her understanding of the reality of defeat. It is the limitation of romantic dreams; the end of the comic banter and the superficial caresses that deceived her in the opening scenes. The truth was in the prophecy to Charmian, 'You shall outlive the lady whom you serve'. In I ii, it distracted Cleopatra and she lost her Emperor. In III xi, she knows that the reality of such words has come nearer, but through understanding this she has also drawn closer to Antony. Their love is no longer superficial.

It was this development which characterised Miss Lapotaire's image of the Queen, growing from frivolity to understanding. The conclusion was not going to be iconic but psychologically naturalistic. Death was to be given the mystique of the monument, but its reality was to be stressed in an emotional manner.

This is first apparent with Antony's death [IV xv]. His loss is presented in a richly modulated manner. The slightly echoing chamber is presented in dark blue, with a steady flow of white incense fumes to the rear. Cleopatra is in white, her hair dishevelled. But she still has some drapes – one multicoloured over her arm, two in red held by Iras and Charmian – with which they are to bring Antony to them. There are also a few cushions, the last remnants of their luxury. The scene opens with her voicing the fear that she will 'never go from hence', continues by her expressing desperation at the loss of Antony, and concludes with her smiling resolve concerning her own death. During this course it raises some pertinent aspects of a television production, particularly of the medium's ability to increase the intensity of the text through the close-up shot.

Jonathan Miller has Antony raised just a few feet to the
monument*, allowing a picture from behind Cleopatra of the
Emperor held aloft by his soldiers. When he is at last in
Cleopatra's arms, the lovers are naturally emphasised in a
single frame as she repeatedly kisses him. The director,
however, briefly switches the shot to have Charmian in view at
her cry of 'O heavy sight'; and then the camera returns to the
lovers. In seeking to achieve such intensity in a television
studio, the production gains more than it loses. The monument
appears plainly unrealistic but, as the camera focuses upon the
lovers, the perennial problems of television performance in
relation to the text disappear. The close-up, by cutting out any
extraneous visual material, liberates the text in a manner
impossible even in the theatre, allowing the visual and the
verbal exactly to match. By focusing on the lovers themselves, it
does what the eye would wish to do in a stage production.

Jonathan Miller keeps the scene without cuts, allowing the
actress to find the pace of the performance from the text itself.
Her voice wavers and cracks as she moves in and out of despair:

> Noblest of men, woo't die?
> Hast thou no care of me? Shall I abide
> In this dull world, which in thy absence is
> No better than a sty? O, see, my women,
> The crown o' th'earth doth melt. My lord!   [IV xv 59–63]

Jane Lapotaire's delivery of these lines lead her to the
culmination of Cleopatra's thoughts – the dreams of what has
been and the realisation of what is – and proves one of the most
emotional moments of the production. For her development
there is one final step, and Miss Lapotaire seizes it at the lines
'then is it sin / To rush into the secret house of death / Ere
death dare come to us?' From total despair a final hope
glimmers, bringing a smile to the distraught face. The scene
ends with a resolution in a new dream, not the one of the
'noblest of men', but of her determination to conduct the final
act of her powerful will. In this way it is she who finally
comforts her women. Miss Lapotaire totally masters the scene.
In a rehearsal programme broadcast a few days before the

---

*See plate 6.

production, even the director was seen to be in tears at the
emotional strength of the performance. It is a fine presentation
of a Shakespearean episode on the television screen, and one
which is in complete harmony with the pace of the text.

The emotional power of the scene develops from the
presentation of Cleopatra's growing understanding of Antony
and her relationship with him. It also stems from her concept of
the Queen's developing strength in a lost situation. The tone
continues through Act v. She is easily beguiled by Proculeius,
struggling powerlessly to be free from his soldiers. The fire of
Lapotaire's Cleopatra is evident here as she pushes her
shoulders and face forward, her eyes darting, her constantly
moving head determinedly expressing her resolve. In her
death, however, she resumes the resignation and strength of her
tragedy. The camera again closes to frame her as she quietly
bares her shoulder and caressingly places the serpent over it
and towards her breast:

> As sweet as balm, as soft as air, as gentle –
> O, Antony!

She breathes heavily in a moment reminiscent of sexual
satisfaction with Antony:

> Nay, I will take thee too.
> What should I stay

– and to the left quietly sinks her head in death: eyes closed,
mouth slightly parted. Through the play Miss Lapotaire
demonstrates therefore the power of Cleopatra, from the gaiety
of laughter to the realisation of failure, to the resolve of death. It
is a movement in the drama which she worked on throughout
the rehearsal period but which she modestly tells us she
discovered only in the final performance before the cameras:

> And the thing I found about Cleopatra – really only on the last day,
> doing the last act – was that she starts off very loud and very fiery
> and very colourfully and extravagantly and eccentrically, and she
> is, in fact, at the beginning of the play a very small human being; by
> the end of the play she becomes a very large human being and she is

reduced in terms of her extravagance by the events and force of circumstances that have happened to her.

(BBC *'Antony and Cleopatra': The Production*, p. 26.)

That small is loud and large, quiet, is the characteristic of her revelatory performance. It is one which complements and contrasts with the beautiful and iconographic appearance of Vivien Leigh, the sexual and political calculation of Janet Suzman, and Glenda Jackson's intimate portrayal of authority in love.

9   ANTONY

Colin Blakely: Jonathan Miller's Television Production, 1980

The theatrical strength of Cleopatra obviously needs to be complemented by her Antony. It is here, however, that problems of staging the play often raise themselves. The relationship between the two characters requires a difficult balance of contrasting temperament which can pose real dilemmas for a casting director. Antony has to be considered in terms of his Cleopatra (or vice versa), of his infatuation, and of his past and present role as commander and Emperor.

In playing Antony to Jane Lapotaire's Cleopatra, Colin Blakely was harshly criticised in the pages of *Shakespeare Quarterly*: 'Of Lilliputian stature . . . and equipped with a scruffy beard, he seems cruelly miscast, not interestingly different' (32, 1981, p. 399). The reviewer desired a more traditional Brobdingnagian representation. Yet Colin Blakely in many respects portrayed a role consistent with Jonathan Miller's overall vision of the work. If, in the opening scenes Cleopatra is a romantic then Antony has to counterpoint her presentation. So, in this interpretation, he is presented, not as an Adonis or as Titania's Ass, but rather as the rugged, tired and disillusioned soldier and intense lover. Duty clearly forces him on, but he longs for a relaxation of the burden. Cleopatra is the old man's attempted escape from his responsibilities, but she is also someone who has totally captured him. The focus of the production is therefore placed on his relationship with her and his difficulty in understanding the demands she makes on him.

In this respect, Miller omitted much of the text which emphasises the political climate outside the immediate relationship. In Act I, scenes ii and iii are reduced so as to present only the bare essentials of Pompey's danger – seventeen lines which exemplify Pompey's grievance, stature and growing popularity being omitted. The emphasis is therefore left with the lovers, who simply do not want to part, whatever the reason. Moreover, the quarrel scene is edited to reduce snide or hurtful remarks. Cleopatra does not satirically refer to Antony as a 'Herculean Roman' [I iii 84]; nor does she taunt him by imitating and pre-empting one of his favourite oaths 'Now, by my sword' – 'And target' [82]; nor does she banter phrases with him, even in her reconciliation as with,

> 'Tis sweating labour
> To bear such idleness so near the heart
> As Cleopatra this. . . .   [93–5]

– but instead comes straight to the point in showing her love for him:

> . . .   But, sir, forgive me;
> Since my becomings kill me when they do not
> Eye well to you. . . .   [95–7]

This Cleopatra is in love with a man who nominally performs his duties to the world but who cares for nothing but their relief. He is no longer the Herculean about to be defeated but one already in defeat, taking refuge in his relationship with a queen. Blakely therefore portrays Antony with lines about his eyes, a coarse beard and a receding hair line. His face is strained with tension and bankrupt desire, while his teeth and eyes are constantly taut with irritation at the world's affairs and his part in them. It is an Antony who cares for Cleopatra tenderly, protectively holding her, but doing so with the distant gaze of the wearied mind. Consequently he gives the intense impression of wishing to be constantly with his love but being drawn away by his reputation. His lust for love can only thinly disguise his deep knowledge of weakness. In such a portrayal Antony misjudges Cleopatra. He fails to understand her final scheme because he has not been able to read the subtlety and sincerity of her character.

His inability to kill himself in a scene set in his war-tent is a characteristic element of the presentation. Bound in by the canvas of the tent and the linen of the bedclothes, he bellows at Eros to kill him and impatiently takes his leave of the servant as he kneels, head bent for self-condemned execution. With Eros's death Antony cries out in impotent fury before holding his servant's head in an attempt at understanding. He then kneels on the bed, falls onto his sword and so to the pillows. Flies are intermittently heard buzzing as if waiting for carrion, and the heat appears to grow more intense as the light shines into the camera, obscuring the faces of the soldiers and Alexas (here given Diomedes's role) who come to his aid. In the white heat, with his head fallen back from the pillows, Blakely's Antony realises the irony of his misjudgement;* but the pain of his wound is also prominent in the yell he gives as the soldiers lift him up.

To the end, Blakely presents the intense lover trying to give his whole being to his love, but he is also the hedonist and the general attempting to flee from the world but failing to break its bonds. It may not be the most satisfying interpretation of the part, but in its realism it is one forming a neat relationship with Cleopatra's growing awareness of her self and the nature of her love and history. In this respect his portrayal tempers any leanings towards sentiment or romanticism. Imagination is allowed its reign, but both characters are made aware of the reality.

Laurence Olivier: Benthall/Olivier Production, 1951

Olivier's Antony thirty years earlier can be seen in total contrast to Blakely's. Olivier was aging but proud, punctilious

---

*See plate 7.

about appearance; hair and clothes in perfect order. He was tired but not bitter, and still possessed a quick wit ready to engage Caesar verbally at the conference table. As such he portrayed 'a man in the process of disintegration, beginning in a rather low key, working up through his childish bravado in the wars to the climax of uncontrolled fury in the scene of irrational jealousy' (Alice Venezky, *Shakespeare Quarterly*, 3, 1952, p. 124).

His was the great façade. Whereas Blakely shows Antony's total weariness throughout, Olivier saw the character as attempting to hide his decline and disillusionment under the disguise of each new enterprise. The grey in the hair, the general nervousness about each piece of news were to be fought, but their existence naturally exposed the declining man beneath. He was enrapt by Cleopatra, 'dallying' with her 'instead of listening to his soldiers' arguments against fighting at sea' (Venezky, p. 124). His infatuation was one not of sentimentality but of doting joviality and good humour which could turn rapidly into intense cruelty, as with the Thidias episode. To some extent, this made the actor vulnerable to charges of histrionics, but such a juxtaposing of emotions does not merely characterise an element of Olivier's style but one also of Elizabethan drama in general. The lesser dramatists, in particular, make effective theatrical moments through blatant contrast. Shakespeare is no exception in this play, and Olivier was alert to the modulations of the text. In his attempted suicide, as Venezky notes, he flung his sword from him as he wounded himself only to find, when not dead, that he could no longer reach it and therefore had to call for help. Resolve and impotency were swiftly and effectively presented.

From great Emperor to amusing lover to cruel tyrant to shamed general to total helplessness, he marked the steps of Antony's decline; but throughout he was aware that there was something lacking in the performance, as Margaret Lamb notes,

> The actor himself felt that he had not completely understood the play and cited as a difficulty 'the lack of character drawing at the beginning of Antony's story'. For Olivier, Antony only partially believed that the actor could reclaim himself (p. 140–2).

Like many of the critics who berated him for not attaining a greater tragic intensity, the actor may well have been hoping too much from the part Shakespeare created. In performance he pushed the role to its limits within a conventional reading of Shakespearean tragedy. He consequently showed neither a Hamlet nor an Othello, but still a great man finally defeated and thereby reduced to total despair. In Act IV, utterly distraught and ashamed with head declined, he weaved through the pillars: a lost Samson unable to achieve his greatest deed. The text asks for no more and Olivier therefore played within his own and Shakespeare's limits. Hence he found in Antony a tragic element which, as *The Times* reported, was exciting and original but not noble. It was this reading which characterised his vision and which stunned the audience into a concentrated silence for his death scene.

Richard Johnson: Trevor Nunn's Production, 1972

Richard Johnson playing opposite Janet Suzman was physically well-built for Antony. He is a tall sturdy man suited to the role of warrior and general. As a Brobdingnagian he employed his stature neatly to contrast with Miss Suzman's vitality and to show his inner dilemma. His stance was determined by his environment, thus making constant visual points for the audience. Peter Thompson recalled:

> In Rome he stood straight, and spoke decisively, as in the assertive quelling of Octavius at 'I am not married, Caesar' [II ii 127]. In Egypt he was slightly stooped, self-consciously aging, the vacillating Antony divided against himself.
>
> (*Shakespeare Survey*, 26, 1973, pp. 146–7.)

He was, however, always a man of authority. He dominated the procession which opened the play, looking round the gloriously coloured heavens of Egypt eagle-eyed and yet content with his Cleopatra. In a long white linen gown, he was the aging though still confident Antony, face wrinkled, beard grizzled and greying. The fall was imminent but had not yet occurred, and thus Johnson presented an attitude of strength in combat with

weariness. When the Actium defeat did come, the canopy of the
court was displayed fallen from the skies, the luxurious
cushions were displaced and Antony appeared broken, at one
with the deranged set. At no time was he seen as a poetic
Antony, the ruggedness being evident throughout the role
whether in Alexandria, Athens or Rome. Thus Nunn's cuts in
the text were such as to reduce embellishment in Antony's
speeches, presenting him rather as the straight-forward and
pragmatic speaker politician and soldier. In the great debate
with Caesar, therefore, such a qualification as 'but mine
honesty / Shall not make poor my greatness, nor my
power / Work without it' [II ii 96–8] was omitted leaving the
main apology:

>   ...   As nearly as I may,
> I'll play the penitent to you; ...
>   ...
>   ...   Truth is that Fulvia,
> To have me out of Egypt, made wars here,
> For which myself, the ignorant motive, do
> So far ask pardon as befits mine honour
> To stoop in such a case.   [II ii 95–6, 98–102]

There was to be no mystery surrounding the man and little
elaboration of thought. Thus his meeting in defeat with
Cleopatra [III xi] was severely reduced, as we have seen Miller
was later to do for Blakely:

EROS   Most noble sir, arise, The Queen approaches.
 . . .
ANT.   O, whither has thou led me, Egypt?
 . . .
CLEO.   O my lord, my lord,
        Forgive my fearful sails! I little thought
        You would have followed.   [III xi 46, 51, 54–6]

Such a directness of approach characterised the man, as he
broke through to the essentials of the situation. What had she
done? Where had she taken him? The tragedy was in the single
line rather than its explanation or expansion. Yet beneath the
simplicity of approach was the Emperor's illusion. As Charles

Lewsen noted (*The Times*, 16 Aug. 1972), Antony's later call for 'one other gaudy night' [III xiii 182] had 'a splendid drive' but one 'underscored by the fact that neither sexual ecstasy nor military greatness is any more possible' to him. The illusion motivated him, but was at the centre of his fall. In his last proposal to Eros [IV xiv], the director cut the speech by ten lines. Antony was to be as plain-speaking as ever:

EROS   What would my lord?
   . . .
ANT.   Thou art sworn, Eros,
       That, when the exigent should come, which now
       Is come indeed, when I should see behind me
       Th' inevitable prosecution of
       Disgrace and horror, that on my command
       Thou then would'st kill me. Do't; the time is come.
   . . .
EROS   The gods withhold me! [IV xiv 55, 62–7, 69]

As Eros made his decision the bantering between him and the general [lines 80–95] was also cut, so that there were no farewells but merely the servant's swift suicide in the face of Antony's stern resolution:

EROS   O, sir, pardon me.
ANT.   When I did make thee free, swor'st thou not then
       To do this when I bade thee? Do it at once,
   . . .
EROS   My sword is drawn.
   . . .
             Shall I strike now?
ANT.   Now, Eros.
EROS   Why, there then! Thus I do escape the sorrow
       Of Antony's death.   [IV xiv 80–2, 88, 93–5]

The tragedy with this direct and honest Antony was that, in the face of his pragmatism, he had become strangely naïve. Innocent, not in poetic illusions nor in escapism, but in his age and its weariness displayed in Egypt, counterfeited in Rome.

Alan Howard: Peter Brook's Production, 1978

The immediately noticeable feature about Alan Howard's
Antony for the Peter Brook production was that he was not the
aging man. He was older than Octavius, but not to the
conventional extent. The dotage of this general was tempered
by a need to find true maturity. Howard presented an Antony
caught more in the trauma of the male menopause than in the
lasciviousness of sexual decadence. That is not to say that he
was not enrapt by the vitality of his Queen, but rather that he
was suffering from a dilemma which demanded love and duty
simultaneously. The love was not a sexual caprice but a
relationship with a woman of 'infinite variety' who would taunt
and chastise him in his dilemma rather than satisfy him in lust.
Consequently, Howard appeared as a red-faced robust Antony
who would flare into a rage and yet chastise himself as he did so
– a man intellectually wracked by his appreciation of his
dilemma.

Nowhere was this trait more apparent than in the Thidias
episode [III xiii 85ff]. As Antony and Enobarbus entered
stage-right, Cleopatra, seated on a large cushion left, was
entertaining Thidias. On the word 'Favours', Thidias stood
and slowly backed away downstage-right in realisation of his
fault. Enobarbus followed him from upstage-right, while
Antony, now upstage-centre, strode downstage-centre.
Antony, on 'Ah, you kite!', crossed around the left side of
Cleopatra, pushing Charmian and Iras aside. In agitation, on
'Have you no ears?', he strode up centre, and with the entry of
the soldiers stage-right he strode once again down centre.
Enobarbus, on 'old one dying', took Thidias's hand while
Antony moved to centre-stage. On 'Whip him, fellows',
Enobarbus delivered Thidias to the soldiers who grabbed him
so as to drag him behind the flats centre-right for an exit left, on
'Take him hence'. Antony meanwhile strode to the centre
entrance and then, on 'You were half blasted ere I knew you',
walked down stage to the right of Cleopatra, just behind her.

These actions flowed from the text. Thidias is the immediate
victim of the Emperor's wrath, but the real object of his anger is
Cleopatra. Thus the striding Antony separated them on stage,
moving from one side to the other and then up and down centre,

giving the impression of an agitated lion wounded on one side
by Caesar's man and on the other more grievously by his love.
Enobarbus kept well clear of him, taking charge of Thidias as
Antony scattered Cleopatra's ladies yelling for his soldiers. In
this ranting mood no one was safe. Cleopatra, however,
remained calm, seated on her cushion, and thus Brook set up a
neat contrast between her stability and Antony's irritated
despondency. As the action continued, the despondency was
shown to be close to despair. With Antony now to the right of
Cleopatra, he crouched down beside her on the words 'Dead
Caesar's trencher', taking her hand on 'My playfellow' and
kneeling by her, only to stand again at 'haltered neck', releasing
her hand in preparation for the reentrance of Thidias at 'about
him'. At this point, Caesar's messenger was brought in from the
left to above centre-left from where he was thrown down right of
Cleopatra. As Antony then moved behind him, Thidias
attempted to slide himself upstage. The rage, however, had not
been quelled and thus, on 'Thou hast been whipped', Antony
grabbed the man and lifted him to his feet only to throw him
down again, on 'Shake thou to look on't', as he moved to the
right of him. He then kicked Thidias at the words 'He may at
pleasure whip', before crossing downstage-right on 'to quit
me'. Thidias left the stage on 'be gone!', while Antony moved to
the corner of the downstage-right screen, where crouching he
cried. Cleopatra now crossed to him and stood to his left,
moving around to his right on 'Not know me yet?'.

The movements here demonstrated Antony's total tragedy.
From the stamping rage with Thidias could be seen the torment
of the political situation. His anger may have been vented at
Caesar's agent and at Cleopatra, but the kneeling by her, the
taking of her hand, the quick movement up again, the kicking of
Thidias and the final collapse in tears illustrated his breakdown
before the grim reality of his love for the Queen as opposed to
his oncoming inevitable defeat by Caesar. He could whip, kick,
rail at Caesar's servants, but his tears showed that he was tied
to Cleopatra and that therefore his political threats were
worthless and ineffective. All that he could hope for was her brief
comfort. She obliged. Standing to the right of him, Cleopatra
proclaimed her innocence. Thus, on 'I am satisfied', they
embraced, Antony bringing her to kneel by him. As he did so

they fell together onto the floor, only for Cleopatra then to kneel upright. Antony knelt to the right of her on 'his fate', while on 'To kiss these lips' they both stood and moved slowly to the centre of the stage. The tension was gradually being relieved so that it could be purged with laughter at Cleopatra's announcement of her birthday. From despair the mood changed to an escapist frivolity as Cleopatra spun round and round, proclaiming 'I will be Cleopatra' before, in giddiness, falling to the floor. Iras and Charmian were sent on the errand to fetch Antony's captains, leaving the centre of the stage for the lovers. Antony lay beside his Queen on 'Come on, my queen', the couple rolling joyfully downstage together. As they stopped at 'I'll make death love me', he lifted Cleopatra on to his shoulders. They then left the stage for Enobarbus.

It was a scene demonstrating in its orchestration the turbulence of Antony's despair in love, the loss of command being replaced by the comfort of the moment. But the irony was present. It was precious moments like these that had caused the events leading to the finality of despair. From such a paradox, what comfort could there be? Enobarbus moved stage-centre to give his commentary:

> Now he'll outstare the lightning. To be furious
> Is to be frighted out of fear, and in that mood
> The dove will peck the estridge; and I see still
> A diminution in our captain's brain
> Restores his heart. When valour preys on reason,
> It eats the sword it fights with. I will seek
> Some way to leave him.   [III xiii 194–200]

Howard's Antony and Brook's orchestration of the scene was in line with this poignant comment by the rough soldier. The frivolity disguised the turbulence of fortune.

In one respect, such a reading of Antony naturally led to critical charges that the performance was external. Yet Antony's role is largely an external one. As we have seen, Olivier found that the Emperor is neither a Hamlet nor an Othello. He does not possess their tragic introspection and is given no soliloquies. He is a man, however, seen in a pattern of circumstances; and although Alan Howard was possibly too greatly influenced by the part of Coriolanus that he was playing in a largely stylised manner at the Aldwych, rationing out his days between London and Stratford, his reading of the part was intelligent if not forceful. It presented yet another variation of the role on the post-war stage.

10 THE FOUR PRODUCTIONS: GENERAL COMPARISONS

In contrasting the four productions we find that, although common elements naturally permeate each, the focus changes significantly. It depends largely on the conception of the lovers: Olivier's tragic fall was understandable in the context of Leigh's quiet beauty; Johnson's aging pragmatist complemented Suzman's sensual politician; Howard's despair discovered a strength in Jackson's calm; Blakely's weary dissolute found refuge in Lapotaire's need for fulfilment. But the lovers are a part of a complex pattern which these days depends largely on directorial decisions.

Analysis of the text, as we have seen, can trace Shakespeare's emphasis on the Venus-Hercules background to the story. No recent production, however, has attempted to bring this aspect to the fore and, indeed, references to the respective gods and major allusions such as 'the shirt of Nessus' have been consistently cut in modern production. Directors may well feel that the imagery no longer works for the modern audience or that an emphasis on the relationship with the gods would be inappropriate to modern society. Certainly, Ron Daniels discovered something similar in his 1982 production of *The Tempest*, in which his presentation of Prospero's spirits appeared not as intended, like figures from an Inigo Jones masque, but as embarrassingly comic refugees from the top of a Christmas tree. Modern sensibility has to be taken into account in directorial decisions, and this has largely resulted in an emphasis, with *Antony and Cleopatra*, on its political contrasts.

The casting of Caesar in particular has become a key decision. To Olivier's broken general Robert Helpmann presented an effete Caesar, sinister stern and tight-lipped, a young and uncompromising god. Corin Redgrave in 1972 was similarly cold but not effete. His Rome was that of the young businessman who had no time for the sexual caprices or manoeuvres of Janet Suzman's Cleopatra. For Peter Brook, Jonathan Pryce played a politician but one not devoid of feelings. He had a warmth for Octavia and also for the robust Antony, whose fall he could not comprehend. Similarly for Jonathan Miller, Ian Charleston is a puzzled Caesar. He constantly screws up his eyes in an attempt to understand the folly of his competitor, but he knows too that he lives in a cynical world. He holds back the tears at Octavia's departure but allows them to fall freely at Antony's death, while still he probes his mind to discover why it had to happen in this way.

In this respect, the characterisation of Caesar has proved more varied than that of Enobarbus, who has been played consistently as the old sweat. Peter Brook, however, interestingly asked Patrick Stewart – who also played the part for Trevor Nunn – to emphasise the choric role of the character. Thus he was often seen downstage talking to the audience, pointing out the significance of the action.

Together the four productions illustrate the complexity of the play. The Cleopatra myth and its tradition demand spectacle. The text is rich in the language of splendour and deity, but its first performance necessarily omitted scenes of great passion or visual pomp. The choice for the modern director has to be between the intimate or the splendid.

Michael Benthall and Trevor Nunn chose the spectacular, employing the mechanics of modern staging to overcome the traditional problems of such productions. In both cases this approach was successful, but the intimacy of the tragedy was lost in the iconography.

Jonathan Miller with the television screen had the opportunity to bring the play into the domesticity of the home. Certain scenes, particularly the death of Antony, worked well; but his decision to set the play for television against the Veronese backcloth was essentially self-destructive. To what extent is Veronese more accessible to modern popular cultural trends than ancient Egypt or Rome or Elizabethan England? More significantly: how can the small screen cope with the sweep of a Veronese canvas? Miller's camera displays the ability to pick out the particular within the vast scope, but the backcloth is unable to be contained and therefore becomes ineffective.

Peter Brook, in contrast, presented his vision of an intimate *Antony and Cleopatra* in the impersonal Royal Shakespeare Theatre rather than the small studio. The result was a fascinating experiment but one which, even though it divided the stage with a screen to bring the action closer to the audience, became lost in the open spaces of the large theatre. Brook demonstrated radical thinking – although that in itself does not guarantee a superior production. He also concentrated on the text for stage progression and therefore omitted less than Benthall, Nunn or Miller. In this respect, Brook showed a faith in Shakespeare which is not always evident in the modern theatre. But in doing so in such an overtly intellectual manner, he lost the vitality displayed in Nunn's 1972 version.

Like the character of Cleopatra, the play is something of an enigma. It can accommodate contrasting interpretations, but as yet it seems to have foiled the modern directors' attempt to encompass in one production its 'infinite variety'.

11   POSTSCRIPT: THE 1982 PRODUCTION

Adrian Noble's Production at The Other Place, *1982*

As this book came to its conclusion, the Royal Shakespeare Company presented a new production of *Antony and Cleopatra* at their studio theatre, with Helen Mirren and Michael Gambon directed by Adrian Noble. This is the first RSC production of the play since Peter Brook's intended-intimate version of 1978, and it therefore could be expected to build on Brook's concept – especially as it is staged in the small theatre. Adrian Noble, however, although stressing the intimacy of the drama, plays against the Brook/Jackson concept.

Miss Mirren's Queen shows neither political authority nor regality in the first four acts, but rather displays a novel

interpretation of a Cleopatra desperate for the love of Antony.*
The 'dotage' of love seems to be completely on her side as, in the
argument [I iii], she furiously moves about the almost bare
stage until, leaning against a wooden support, she comes near
to mental collapse. She pauses while the quiet emotion wells up
in her for the most tender expression of her love, 'Courteous
lord, one word . . .'.

In these opening scenes Miss Mirren's is a highly moving
portrayal of a woman in love and she is complemented by a
towering, controlled Antony, brim-full of authority. From the
moment they first enter stage-right, her eyes covered by a silver
scarf held at some distance behind by the Emperor, we see the
frivolity and blindness of love with her, the reins with him.
When Michael Gambon's Antony speaks, we hear a voice
which is strong, rich and cultivated. Cleopatra's desperation
for this eloquent and authoritative man's love produces
moments of great dramatic power – as when, on hearing of his
marriage, she flares into the usual temper but also sadly
doubles herself up, holding her stomach as she moans 'He's
married . . . He's married'.

Difficulties ensue, however, from the decision to place
Cleopatra's regality to one side. Unless she is consistently the
Queen, her 'infinite variety' can come dangerously close to
inconsistency. Helen Mirren plays the Thidias episode as a
strumpet, seductively lying against Charmian's back whilst,
glancing at the entering Antony, she teases him by blatantly
flirting with Caesar's man. Antony's answer is to strike her to
the floor* and later straddle her as she were a whore. It is
difficult to reconcile this Cleopatra with the shrouded dream
vision which appears to Antony after the surrender of the fleet;
or with the ashen begrimed widow, from Plutarch, locked in her
monument with the bloodied winding sheet of her dead
Emperor. Each interpretation is powerful, but in its early days
the production had not reconciled itself with the others or with
an overall conception of the play.

Similarly, it is hard to reconcile Gambon's authoritative
presence with the futility of his fall. As Irving Wardle has
noted: 'We see the two partners losing each other in the process

---

*See plates 2 and 8, respectively.

of losing power. There is no real alternative between love and politics, and in this case the world is not well lost' (*The Times*, 15 Oct. 1982). It is a pity that the old question of 'the world well lost' raises itself again, but this seems inevitable from the progress of the production. Michael Gambon's Antony becomes more and more externalised, with phrases such as 'Hark! The land bids me tread no more upon't' [III xi 1] being uttered in soft tones, and the death scene handled with a detached objectivity. Thus 'I am dying, Egypt' becomes a matter-of-fact statement rather than a moment of great emotion.

In this respect, Bob Peck's Enobarbus complements the production with the presentation of an unpoetic malcontent more appropriate perhaps to Shakespeare's *Troilus and Cressida* or to a play by Marston or Middleton. Likewise, Jonathan Hyde's Octavius Caesar plays against the politically cold interpretation of recent years in showing a man himself almost in love with Antony. He leans from the upper tier of the dual-level set to call on the Antony of the lower Egyptian world to release himself from its lascivious snares. Later he is prepared to hug Antony and kiss him at the departure of Octavia. His tears appear genuine, but the attitude is hard to reconcile with the man who will destroy his 'competitor' or plan Cleopatra's humiliation.

Adrian Noble's production, in what is here necessarily a first impression, is one highly charged in the immediacy of certain episodes but lacking in the totality of the vision. As such, it loses power where Brook's gained, but gains where Brook's lost.

READING LIST

EDITIONS

The edition used throughout has been that by Emrys Jones, New Penguin Shakespeare (1977). This contains an excellent introduction to the play. Other editions include J. Dover Wilson, New Cambridge (1950); M. R. Ridley – based on R. M. Case's of 1906 and 1930 – New Arden (1954); Barbara Everett, Signet (1964); and John Ingledew, New Swan Shakespeare Advanced Series (1971). There is also the BBC TV Shakespeare edition (1981).

SOURCES AND BACKGROUND

Geoffrey Bullough, *Narrative and Dramatic Sources of Shakespeare*, V (London, 1964), gives the most detailed collection of sources. T. J. B. Spencer, *Shakespeare's Plutarch* (Harmondsworth, 1964) is a handier volume. I have used this for quotations. Kenneth Muir, *The Sources of Shakespeare's Plays* (London, 1977), includes a chapter on *Antony and Cleopatra*. The standard work written on the Roman plays in the first half of this century was M. W. MacCallum, *Shakespeare's Roman Plays and Their Background* (London, 1910). This was reprinted in 1967, with an introduction by T. J. B. Spencer. It is still very useful. The late T. J. B. Spencer also wrote the informative bibliographical essay in *Shakespeare: Select Bibliographical Guide*, edited by Stanley Wells (London, 1973).

CRITICAL ESSAYS AND STUDIES

The Macmillan Casebook on the play, edited by John Russell Brown (London, 1968), has a good selection of essays; it includes major material by A. C. Bradley, H. Granville-Barker, John Middleton Murry, Maurice Charney, L. C. Knights, John Holloway and H. A. Mason, and it also reprints a selection of theatre reviews, including notices on Edith Evans and Godfrey Tearle (1947), Vivien Leigh and Laurence Olivier (1951), Peggy Ashcroft and Michael Redgrave (1953). I am particularly indebted to Margaret Lamb's *Antony and Cleopatra on the English Stage* (London and Toronto, 1980) which gives a full survey of productions from Shakespeare's day to Peter Brook, 1978. Books and critical essays to which I am also grateful to acknowledge a debt, and which are useful for further study by the reader, include:

John Bayley, *Shakespeare and Tragedy* (London, 1981).

S. L. Bethell, *Shakespeare and the Popular Dramatic Tradition* (London, 1944).

John Russell Brown, *Discovering Shakespeare: A New Guide to the Plays* (London and Basingstoke, 1981; reprinted 1983) – see for a consideration of the theatricality of the plays.

Lord David Cecil, *'Antony and Cleopatra'* in *Poets and Storytellers* (London, 1949).

Maurice Charney, *Shakespeare's Roman Plays: The Function of Imagery in Drama* (Cambridge, Mass. 1961). This is an excellent extended study of the way in which Shakespeare's imagery functions thematically in the plays by both stimulating and complementing dramatic action.

David Daiches, 'Imagery and Meaning in *Antony and Cleopatra*', in *Modern Literary Essays* (Edinburgh, 1968).

John F. Danby, *Poets on Fortune's Hill* (London, 1952); reprinted as *Elizabethan and Jacobean Poets* (London, 1964) – see for further reference to Mars and Venus.

Richard David, *Shakespeare in the Theatre* (London, 1978) – see, in particular, for an account of the 1972 production.

Madeleine Doran, *Shakespeare's Dramatic Language* (Madison, Wisconsin, 1976).

Northrop Frye, *Fools of Time: Studies in Shakespearean Tragedy* (Toronto, 1967).

T. Hallin, 'Jonathan Miller on the Shakespeare Plays', in *Shakespeare Quarterly*, 32 (1981).

Terence Hawkes, *Shakespeare's Talking Animals* (London, 1972).

E. A. J. Honigmann, *Shakespeare, Seven Tragedies: The Dramatist's Manipulation of Response* (London and Basingstoke, 1976).

Emrys Jones, *Scenic Form in Shakespeare* (London, 1971).

G. Wilson Knight, *The Imperial Theme* (London, 1951).

Dorothea Krook, *Elements of Tragedy* (New Haven, Conn., 1969).

F. R. Leavis, *'Antony and Cleopatra* and *All For Love*: A Critical Exercise', in *Scrutiny*, 5 (1936–7).

Michael Lloyd, 'Cleopatra as Isis', in *Shakespeare Survey*, 12 (1959).

Maynard Mack, 'The Jacobean Shakespeare', *Stratford-upon-Avon Studies*, 1 (London, 1960).

D. R. C. Marsh, *Passion Lends Them Power* (Manchester, 1976).

E. Schanzer, *The Problem Plays of Shakespeare* (London, 1963).

G. B. Shaw, Preface, *Three Plays for Puritans* (Penguin, 1946). This volume includes Shaw's *Caesar and Cleopatra*.

J. L. Simmons, *Shakespeare's Pagan World: The Roman Tragedies* (Charlottesville, Va., 1973).

J. I. M. Stewart, *Character and Motive in Shakespeare* (London, 1949).

Terence Spencer, 'Shakespeare and the Elizabethan Romans', in *Shakespeare Survey*, 10 (Cambridge 1957) – see this volume also for J. C. Maxwell's review of critical works on the Roman plays, 1900–1956 and for W. M. Merchant, 'Classical Costume in Shakespearian Productions'.

Theodore Spencer, *Shakespeare and the Nature of Man* (New York, 1942).

Brents Stirling, *Unity in Shakespearian Tragedy* (New York, 1956).

D. A. Traversi, *Shakespeare: The Roman Plays* (London, 1963).

mostly
Blank verse — no couplets
very *few* soliloquies. *some prose.*
78   READING LIST

E. M. Waith, *The Herculean Hero in Marlowe, Chapman, Shakespeare and Dryden* (New York, 1962).

John Wilders, *The Lost Garden: A View of Shakespeare's English and Roman History Plays* (London and Basingstoke, 1978; reprinted 1982).

changes past tense to present.

Antony's infatuation is undisputable, but what about Cleo — is it all a game to her.

After all, flirts with Caesars messenger.

+ only killed herself rather than be captured

This sums up the situation throughout the play, which is full of paradoxes, which reflect the confused state of Antony's mind. The tragedy + comedy contradictions within the plays are also manipulated to this end.

was it witchcraft / wasn't it - not clear.
as it wasn't / or not?
as it right or wrong?

INDEX OF NAMES

tall, aging

status.

decline

tidier in appearance
with Cleo.

careless in appearance
in Rome. tall —to match
Antony's status.

Cleo — should always
look regal + immaculate
(colour purple somewhere in there)

By suffering both political and
personal defeat, her authority
was in question.

royal + sensual.